The Roads Taken

The University of Georgia Press   Athens & London

Fred Setterberg

THE
ROADS
TAKEN

TRAVELS

THROUGH

AMERICA'S

LITERARY

LANDSCAPES

© 1993 by Fred Setterberg

All rights reserved

Published by the University of Georgia Press

Athens, Georgia 30602

Designed by Louise OFarrell

Set in 10/14 Sabon

by Tseng Information Systems, Inc.

Printed and bound by Braun-Brumfield, Inc.

The paper in this book meets the guidelines for
permanence and durability of the Committee
on Production Guidelines for Book Longevity
of the Council on Library Resources.

Printed in the United States of America

97   96   95   94   93   C   5   4   3   2   1

Library of Congress Cataloging in Publication Data

Setterberg, Fred.

The roads taken : travels through America's literary
 landscapes / Fred Setterberg.

p. cm.

ISBN 0–8203–1517–6 (alk. paper)

1. Literary landmarks—United States.   2. Authors,
 American—Homes and haunts—United States.
 3. Setterberg, Fred—Journeys—United States.
 I. Title.

PS141.S46   1993

810'.9—dc20

92-38775

British Library Cataloging in Publication Data
available

for Ann

The United States themselves are essentially the greatest poem.

—Walt Whitman, Preface to *Leaves of Grass*

~~~~~~

Where are we going, Walt Whitman?
The doors close in an hour.
Which way does your beard point tonight?

—Allen Ginsberg, "A Supermarket in California"

CONTENTS

xiii ～ Acknowledgments

1 ～ Rising from Jack Kerouac's Couch

17 ～ We Travel Texas Lonesome

44 ～ Underneath Willa Cather's Nebraska

62 ～ Roughing the Truth with Mark Twain

88 ～ Into Some Wild Places with Hemingway

104 ～ Zora Neale Hurston in the Land of 1,000 Dances

132 ～ "Moose. . . Maine . . . Thoreau . . ."

150 ～ My Father's Jack London

ACKNOWLEDGMENTS

For much good advice and encouragement, I would like to thank Les Hodge, Marshall Krantz, Gena Corea, Jimmy Maconochie, Susan Felter, Martha Spaulding, John Raeside, Mary-Helen Burnison, Marilyn Waterman, Diane Newton, Stan Lindberg, and John and Susan Daniel. I am particularly indebted to Anne Fox and Lonny Shavelson for their intelligence, hard work, and wisdom. And to Ann Van Steenberg, I owe more than I can say or probably know. . . .

The Roads Taken

RISING FROM
JACK KEROUAC'S COUCH

I was halfway across America, at the dividing line
between the East of my youth and the West of my future,
and maybe that's why it happened right there and then.

—Jack Kerouac, *On the Road*

"Jack Kerouac slept on that sofa," I announced in the morning.

Wally, my nineteen-year-old cousin, bolted upright from his lethargic sprawl across the appalling wreck of my apartment's ratty red-velvet, cat-clawed couch. Wally's backpack, hiking boots, and cardboard hitch-hiking sign—upon which he had scrawled in coal-black marker pen with excellent penmanship, CALIFORNIA—had been strewn across my Oakland flat since his arrival the night before. I negotiated a path through the debris of my cousin's vagabond life and forced a cup of steaming black coffee into his hand.

Wally gasped, shook his head, slurped the coffee; he couldn't believe it. "*This* sofa?" It was as though I had confided that the lumpy cushions plopped upon this wretched heap of furniture had been stuffed with twenty-dollar bills to soften his sleep.

"Kerouac crashed *here*?" Wally wondrously patted the extruding springs.

Even to me the uncomfortable couch seemed a remarkable prize. I had acquired it years before from a friend whose father had been—I know this sounds unlikely—a Buddhist monk; he'd briefly tutored Gary Snyder, Allen Ginsberg, and Alan Watts in the rigors of Zen. The time was the mid-1950s; the place, Berkeley; the literary epoch, the San Francisco Poetry Renaissance; ergo: Kerouac. My friend recalled that, as a little girl, she had seen red wine spilt and the veil of illusion called *maya* contemplated broodily in her family's living room, as the famous writer nodded off on the couch.

Wally really dug the idea of sleeping where Kerouac had also sprawled. My cousin had arrived after thumbing across the country from Massachusetts, materializing at my door like a spirit from another era. Although we had already hit the end of the eighties, Wally wore sixties buckskin, blue jeans, and shoulder-length hair. In the top flap of his army surplus backpack, he transported an eccentric collection of forgotten music culled not from his own youth, but mine: Blue Cheer, Moby Grape, Iron Butterfly, the Seeds.

A few days after his arrival, while we were driving together through San Francisco, I mentioned to Wally that on the summer solstice twenty years before, I had attended a free concert in Golden Gate Park featuring the original incarnation of the Grateful Dead—a band whom I would now pay only to avoid.

"Damn!" said Wally.

"What's wrong?"

"I missed everything."

Although my young cousin certainly had missed vintage Dead by twenty years and the Beats by thirty-five, he seemed determined to mine from the past a full stock of recyclable wisdom and experience. Most serviceable was the dog-eared paperback stuffed into his backpack. It hardly needs to be said, but Wally was reading Jack Kerouac's *On the Road*.

"That's so weird," he confided on that first morning in Oakland, upon hearing the news about my couch. "That's wickedly weird, in fact, because you know what?" Wally spoke just above a whisper, running his long, thin fingers through his sandy-blonde hair. "I was *born* on October 21, 1969."

I didn't get it.

"The day Jack Kerouac died."

Together we contemplated all possible manifestations of Jack Kerouac's disembodied spirit now hovering above the sacred couch.

~~~~~~

I'd also read *On the Road*—but twenty years earlier, when I was about Wally's age.

Since then, I've been informed by friends and acquaintances equipped with advanced degrees in English literature and graduate seminar training in semiotics, hermeneutics, deconstructionist dialectics, and feminist Marxist analysis that *On the Road* is really about the true meaning of traffic signals and mileage signs posted along Interstate 80, or the passivity of the American male, or the postwar expropriation of travel as a leisure commodity, or perhaps even nothing at all.

All along I thought it was about a couple of schmoes who roll around the continent like two marbles on a tray, goofing on the scenery and enjoying themselves.

In truth, over the years the specifics of the novel had almost faded from memory. I now associated *On the Road* with other early reading pleasures, like *The Willie Mays Story* or the first thirty-one volumes of the Hardy Boys mystery series: books I had once loved that probably wouldn't stand up to reexamination. The idea propounded by my more serious and scholarly friends that *On the Road* is a "text"—a term that conjures up visions of seventh-grade social studies taught with a five-pound primer titled something like *The American People in Their Melting Pot*—implied that the immensely untidy novel contained some central, distillable lesson that, to be extracted, required its corpus to be drugged and dissected. I didn't like to think in that way about books I had once felt strongly about. I knew the old saw about an identical fate awaiting both a dissected frog and a dissected joke (they both die), and I think I feared that this observation might also pertain to the books I had absorbed into my central nervous system as a kid.

Yet even twenty years ago, I had been able to discern, along with thousands of other young and equally undiscriminating readers, at least one worthwhile lesson from Kerouac's best novel: America was worth getting out to take a look at. "All I wanted to do was sneak out into the night and disappear somewhere," shouted Kerouac, echoing my own sentiments, "and go and find out what everybody was doing all over the country."

Reading *On the Road* back then encouraged me to do just that. I imagined myself enlisting in what Kerouac called the "great rucksack revolution" in which "thousands or even millions of young Americans" dashed about helter-skelter to "hear the voices crying in the wilderness, to find the ecstasy of the stars, to find the dark mysterious secret of the origin of faceless wonderless crapulous civilization." I think most of us were fired by more modest ambitions—a mere itch to visit an uncle in

Flint, Michigan, or vague notions about seeing the ocean for the first time. But how could we not learn one or two lessons along the way?

Now twenty years have passed. My nineteen-year-old cousin has turned up at my door like the Ghost of Journeys Forgotten. And I must admit that I've grown lead-footed about travel. As bad, I'm reluctant to open any book—Kerouac or otherwise—that might compel me to rise off the Beat sofa. And yet, under duress, I must sometimes travel around the country for my work. I am a free-lance writer, which is to say that in the eyes of most of my friends I am unemployed, except that I can't collect unemployment insurance. When I travel today, it is often with a skinflint spirit; I am a lifetime away from the young man who routinely set his compass by the books he had just read.

I recall one evening long ago, when I was very young and as far from home as I had ever been, fresh from a long bout of reading the Beats. I was hitching along the coast highway in southern Italy with a thousand-pound rucksack strapped to my back. I hadn't eaten or washed for several days, contributing perhaps to the reluctance of Italian drivers to stop and stuff me and my mountainous pack into their speeding toy Fiats. And so I decided to jump a freight train, as the men in my family had done during the Great Depression—and as Jack Kerouac seemed to be urging me to do from the centrifugal swirl of my bottomless pack, where I had stored rain-swollen editions of *The Dharma Bums*, *Desolation Angels*, and, of course, *On the Road*.

Around dusk, I slipped into the train yard. Two Italian guards immediately breezed out of the weed patch and arrested me.

"You are very stupid," said the head guard in flawless English, spotting me instantly for another of the lumbering young Americans who'd been swarming all summer throughout southern Italy like black flies with backpacks. "It is very dangerous in here."

I agreed that I was stupid, explained that I was sorry, (left out the fact that I had been reading Kerouac), and promised to return to my post at the highway where I would continue to hitchhike until I was transported somewhere very far away.

"Not yet," ordered the head guard, as I tried to saunter off. His accomplice held my arm.

Soon the three of us were strolling down to the station house for a nice talk with the chief engineer.

"*Vous êtes très bête*," the chief engineer told me. "*C'est dangereux ici.*"

"*Oui*," I admitted in my best high school French, proclaiming my regrets, agreeing that I was *un fou*, a real American knucklehead, and that my accent was terrifying.

"Not yet," ordered the head guard. He stalked off, returning minutes later with the brakeman, who conveyed, I guess, the same message in German. I tried to explain that I had got the point in the first two languages, but I didn't speak German.

"Not yet," ordered the head guard. He picked up the telephone and barked out an order in furious Italian.

Shortly another uniformed man appeared at the office door, gasping for breath after his sprint down the platform. He glowered at me, wheezing with asthmatic rage.

I didn't understand a word he said.

"He's speaking Russian," explained the head guard. "Very fluent Russian. Before he worked with us here in the railroad, he sold Italian wines to the Communists. He also speaks Croatian and Czech. You may go now."

I wandered down the road as the skies darkened with rain, full of wonder for the vulnerability of young travelers and convinced that life will often twist and gibber as implausibly as any book. But I had not yet discovered that the weirdest and most implausible nation of all time and directions was my own.

Many of us grossly misinterpreted Kerouac on first perusal, taking his books as an incitement to rush off to foreign shores. In truth, Kerouac was like a lost waif overseas; he was forced to declare himself indelibly, pugnaciously American. The strangest stories could be heard at home.

"The only people for me," says Sal Paradise, the narrator of *On the Road*, "are the mad ones, the ones who are mad to live, mad to talk, mad to be saved, desirous of everything at the same time, the ones who never yawn or say a commonplace thing, but burn, burn, burn like fabulous yellow roman candles exploding like spiders across the stars."

Now that sounds pretty good when you're a kid taking off on your own for the first time, brimming over with expectations for everybody you'll meet along the way. But it's also responsible for the miseries of ten thousand miles. What Kerouac neglected to tell his readers—particularly naive young men like myself for whom reading *On the Road* was like unwrapping a bale of flypaper, its intimations of adventure sticking to our fingers and thumbs and bundling us up into a jumble of romantic illusions that often took years to unravel—was how trying and tedious the road could be.

Historian Daniel Boorstin has aptly pounced upon the etymological roots of the word "travel," binding it to the notion of "travail"—a word derived "from the Latin *tripalium*, a torture instrument consisting of three stakes designed to rack the body." In French, *travail* can mean work or woe, which must have been clear both experientially and linguistically to the French-speaking Canuck Kerouac. "The soul is no traveler," warned Emerson, Kerouac's fellow–New Englander, one hundred years earlier, "the wise man stays at home. . . . Traveling is the fool's paradise."

When my cousin Wally arrived at my Oakland flat, we fell all over each other with talk of our own roadside glimmers of paradise. We disgorged *all* our stories. I insisted on telling Wally all about the year long ago when I hit the road the hardest—starting off by twining up the Grapevine to Los Angeles with six other guys in the back of a flatbed truck, which suddenly caught fire when I flicked a smouldering butt across the straw-stuffed mattresses strapped to the frame. Wally spoke plaintively of standing in the rain for three days straight, failing to hitchhike out of Bellingham, Washington, because he was too wet and ridiculous to be picked up by anybody except Charles Manson. I recalled the pup tent I used throughout a winter in the water-logged Pacific Northwest as it leaked through the top-seam stitching, but held tight at the bottom in a three-inch greasy puddle like a miniature Doughboy swimming pool. I rambled on about spending a sleepless night in a barmaid's bedroom above a cowboy honky-tonk in Carson City, Nevada, while the lady noisily made love to a depressed steel guitar player whose Hawaiian band had been unaccountably engaged for a disastrous three-week gig. Wally said he'd passed the night fitfully in Greyhound bus stations in the worst quarters of New Orleans, Birmingham, Shreveport, and Des Moines (where Kerouac claimed to have found the most beautiful women in the country, but Wally only got moved along in the morning by a garrulous policeman with cigar-stub breath and a porcupine disposition). I remembered sleeping dreamlessly, at last, in a public urinal outside of Duluth. Wally said he'd been waylaid into eight hours of conversation about Jesus across the breadth of Alberta with a sadistic divinity student who kept playing his lone John Prine cassette tape over and over and over and over and. . . . And we both could talk all night about fighting madly above the roar of countless eighteen-wheelers for some means of keeping awake an exhausted truck driver who threatened to fade into an amphetamine blur and run us off the highway; or wobbling down the road on foot with the weight of the Rockies perched upon our shoulders, as cretinous teenagers showered us with empty beer bottles from their speeding family station wagons; or playing the sucker, again and again, as we chased the promising VW minivan (some are still running today) that pulled to the side to pick up hitchers, but then changed its mind at the last second, as the driver gunned his engine, howled like a jackal, and tore off into what the rhapsodic Kerouac incessantly called "the sad and lonely American night."

Not very much had changed since Kerouac hit the road in the late 1940s, followed by me in the late 1960s—and then my cousin at the end of the 1980s.

Of course, Jack Kerouac had not in any strict, actionable sense directed me, Wally, or anybody else to ricochet around America's least exotic locales (Oakland, Detroit, Knoxville, Kalamazoo) as the preferred adventure of our youth. In fact, Kerouac bridled under his designation during the 1960s by *Time* as "the hippie Homer." But *On the Road* is so full of promises about the romance of America on the run (Shelton, Nebraska; Dalhart, Texas; Fresno, California) that we had all somehow skipped over the plentiful passages in which Kerouac copped to "the beat and evil days that come to young guys" who stray far and long from home. When you're fit and callow and susceptible to every kind of illusion as to some maniac virus—including the illusions of literature—you find yourself constantly infected by your own worst judgment, only to be rescued again and again by the ceaseless kindness of strangers.

Back then, twenty years ago, standing by the side of the road in the rain, I always swore that at some future date I would not revise my miseries in order to make them sound more palatable, or worse, *romantic*. But once Wally and I started swapping road stories, as breathless and frantic as Dean Moriarity and Sal Paradise, as self-conscious as countless thousands of other road-ridden travelers who pictured themselves to be

bright reflections of Kerouac and Cassady, I couldn't help realizing that
we were doing exactly that. Here we were, yammering on about best
rides and worst rides and generally stretching the truth like old soldiers.

I just had to tell Wally about the night a buddy and I caught a ride
near Buffalo with an off-duty factory guard who was draining two six-
packs on his way home from work. The drunkard asked me to drive,
and after he'd finished his last Budweiser and passed out in the passenger's seat, I drove all the way to Syracuse, about 130 miles out of
his way. I yacked until midnight about the coldest night of the year in
Toronto, when I stole into an unlocked laundromat to sneak a luxurious
sleep curled up next to the clothes dryers. Wally had already dozed off
upon my Jack Kerouac couch, but I kept blithering away about the air-
conditioned tour bus that once picked me up along California's coast
highway en route to Santa Cruz. The driver had dropped off his paying
passengers at Fisherman's Wharf and then cruised down Highway 1 to
load up the company vehicle with fifty long-haired kids carrying packs
on their backs.

He must have been reading Kerouac too.

~~~~~~

Librarians, school teachers, civil libertarians, and other good and necessary people often claim that nobody is ever seduced by a book—but,
of course, they're dead wrong.

Any book worth opening threatens to divert us from more serious
business; almost any day, I'd rather be reading than working. We're
drawn to the intoxications of our endless stories as though sucking upon
a bottomless wine sack while sprawled under the summer's blooming
shade trees sans appointment calendar, sans answering machine, sans
everything.

But books don't merely provide a cover for a lifetime of lassitude.

We read books, particularly when we're young, because they seduce us with possibilities for mistakes that we haven't yet imagined. It's the best books that serve as manuals for screwing up our lives or resurrecting them or pitting us against the status quo—which is why the book burners begin their crusades by immolating the better writers, instead of the equally flammable but less persuasive works of Sidney Sheldon and Judith Krantz.

Somewhere in heaven there must be a roll book tabulating all the insipid fistfights inspired by reading Norman Mailer at a vulnerable moment, all the unnecessary shots of bourbon gulped down by young men in blind tribute to Jake Barnes and Philip Marlowe, all the young women's heads that might have been kept out of kitchen ovens, except for an ill-timed perusal of *The Bell Jar*.

Kerouac himself was nearly ruined by literature even before he began to write it. In 1944, capping off his career as a Columbia dropout, he helped deposit down a sewer grate the bloody Boy Scout knife that his friend, Lucien Carr, had used to kill a man who'd been trying to seduce him. Although Carr handed himself over to the police and pleaded self-defense, Kerouac was arrested as an accessory after the fact. He was soon released, but the incident sparked rough talk throughout New York City about the pernicious influence of poets: one newspaper had run a photo of Lucien Carr toting into jail copies of Rimbaud's *A Season in Hell* and Yeats's *A Vision*.

Today Jack Kerouac himself stands among the best of the bad influences. And *On the Road* still sells enough copies each year to sustain the author's worst habits, had he managed to survive them.

So when Wally departed from my flat for a couple of days to ride the Greyhound down to Big Sur—where Kerouac had in 1960 executed a drunken seven-hour stomp along the highway and finally sworn off hitchhiking for good (the man *was* thirty-eight years old!)—I spread myself across the historic but still hideous red-velvet, cat-clawed couch, picked up my cousin's copy of *On the Road*, and delved into Kerouac for the first time in twenty years.

The first thing I noticed was how much of the good stuff remained.

On the Road still read like a sweet, sad, fitfully funny book ready to explode with what Kerouac's Beat colleague John Clellon Holmes called "that bottled eagerness," the peculiar blend of innocence and impatient expectation that turns parties into brawls, casual longing into operatic love affairs, disaster into adventure—and always sounds better in recollection than when you're living it at the time.

"The characteristic note struck by Kerouac is exuberance," admitted Norman Podhoretz, perhaps the novel's harshest, most un-Beat critic back in the 1950s. And even today the book's wild, careening energy can jumpstart incipient urges to take off, move, go—even for a middle-aged, immobilized reader like myself. ("Now we must all get out and dig the river and the people and smell the world," insists Dean Moriarity. "He was so excited it made me cry," says Sal Paradise. "Where would it all lead?")

Where it would all lead was, in fact, the cause of some distress among the nation's sedentary literati when *On the Road* was published in 1957.

The earliest newspaper reviews greeted the book's appearance as a "historic occasion," but this flicker of generous praise was quickly extinguished by scorn and sneering from all the higher bastions of letters. In the *New Yorker*, John Updike mocked the novel with a cruel parody titled "On the Sidewalk," in which a vagabond five-year-old tears around a "sad backyard" in "the American noon" on his scooter. Truman Capote uttered his famous televised wisecrack to David Susskind that Kerouac's books weren't writing, but typing. And in its Sunday books section, the *New York Times* eventually neutralized its initial acclaim, dourly noting that the novel actually chronicled "a road . . . that leads nowhere—and which the novelist cannot afford to travel more than once."

And to be honest, twenty years later, sprawled upon my Kerouac couch with no intention whatsoever of taking to the road again (or at least not traveling in a manner that would lead me to sleeping quarters in a public urinal outside of Duluth), I thought that they might have a point.

It's just that I didn't much care.

Yes, it was too painfully evident that the characters were hopelessly confused ("What I accomplished by coming to Frisco I don't know"). And that they were lost (". . . all this franticness and jumping around. We've got to go someplace, find something"). Too often, they were even sentimental ("But no matter, the road is life"). And I felt it impossible to skirt the obvious conclusion that Sal Paradise was a stone loser ("I forgave everybody, I gave up, I got drunk") and that Dean Moriarity was exactly the sort of sociopath that you wanted to avoid along any road ("He only stole cars for joy rides"). But I really didn't care.

Kerouac had kept me reading as a kid: I owed him that much.

What did bother me, however, was that for all of *On the Road*'s speed, motion, and distance consumed ("1,180 miles, in exactly seventeen hours, not counting two hours in the ditch . . . and two with the police in Newton, Iowa.") poor old Dean Moriarity, his buddy Sal Paradise—and, let's face it, Jack Kerouac—didn't actually *see* very much of the country along the way.

What did America look like in 1947 and 1949 when these characters were ping-ponging between the coasts?

Judging from the novel, the United States must have been composed entirely of bus stations, truckstops, and the endless black snake of the highway. The road traveled by Sal, Dean, and Jack seems denuded of its scenery; people along the highway flit by like crows on a wire, and even the nation's breath-robbing monuments of earth, sky, and water—the Rockies, the plains, the Mississippi—flash past with the indifference of typography laid across the printed page. Upon completing the novel for the second time in twenty years, it seemed to me that "the vastness of old tumbledown holy America from mouth to mouth and tip to tip" added up to one marvelous blur.

And in that instant of sheepish recognition—like the moment in a dream when you're about to address a huge lecture hall that contains everybody in the world whom you wish most to impress, but then you suddenly realize that for some reason you're dressed in Nitwit the Clown's polka-dot boxer shorts and propeller-beanie instead of your own most dignified gray suit—I knew that I too had somehow missed the point; in fact, I'd missed the country.

And I figured it was Jack Kerouac's fault.

Wally knew better.

After a few months on the West Coast, my cousin finally wandered back East, found he couldn't stay put, and drifted up toward Alaska. He and a buddy bought a clunky AMC Hornet and shared the driving, like Sal and Dean, like Kerouac and Cassady—but with a crucial difference. When the Hornet clunker's fuel pump failed somewhere in the emptiness of the Yukon, they didn't turn back frantically, they didn't desert each other, or go crazy, or get drunk and give up. They hunkered down for a day and a half and jerry-rigged the necessary repair. Then they pushed on to their destination, up the highway from Eagle Plains to the Arctic Circle. Wally had always wanted to step over the line that officially demarcates the extreme north (the sign, he said, had read: LAT. 66, 33′ N) just to say he'd been there, that he'd seen it.

"It's the farthest I've ever been," he told me one evening, calling from a telephone booth in Anchorage, where he and his buddy had just landed malodorous jobs in a salmon cannery. "But I still want to go farther."

I unfurled myself across the Kerouac couch and listened enviously to every word. And while Wally was rambling on heatedly about the curl of the horns on a Dall sheep ram and the distinguishing hump of the grizzly he'd spotted between Haines Junction and Destruction Bay, and the abandoned gold-fever cabins near Whitehorse, and the four-day outdoors ordeal that he and his buddy had executed along the Chilkoot Pass in British Columbia, I found myself thinking about all the places that I had managed to miss. I knew how Wally must picture me: slabbed across the Kerouac couch with no intention of walking out the front door toward some more demanding adventure, satisfied that I'd already done my vagrant duty. And we both knew that if I hadn't hit the road twenty years earlier, my entire world would probably now be circumscribed by my own neighborhood's sad backyards in the American noon. Far less than he, I had needed somebody to tell me to get up and go.

"I think you should be grateful," insisted Wally, urging me to get up and go again. "Now that you're done reading, don't you want to take another look?"

Sometimes it's hard to explain life and literature to the young; I was forced to use the word *mimesis* twice even though I'm not really sure what it means. I offered to quote extensively from Norman Podhoretz's defamatory essay on Jack Kerouac while Wally held on and paid for the call.

But I couldn't avoid the truth: Wally wasn't only a better traveler than I; he was a superior reader, smart enough not to get stuck in his own favorite stories. For him, they were just someplace to start.

"Well, Wally," I admitted, "maybe in a small way, you've got just the slightest point. I think I'm going to settle down now and take another look at *Desolation Angels*, or *The Dharma Bums*, or *The Subterraneans*, and see what they have to say."

But on the other end of the line, somewhere in a telephone booth in Anchorage, Alaska, Wally had already hung up and moved on. And I knew then that I needed to get out and see the places that I had been mostly reading about for years. I vowed that this time I would not miss the country that stood between my books and the real, hard, sprawling world outside.

WE TRAVEL TEXAS LONESOME

The country talked quiet; one
human voice could drown it out.

—Larry McMurtry, *Lonesome Dove*

When I spotted Lonny staggering past security and through the arrival
gate at the Dallas–Fort Worth airport, I swaggered over to greet him
with a hardy Texas slap on the back and a boisterous cowpoke hoot.

Well, howdy, pardner!

Lonny peered up at me like a bad-tempered pack mule. His back
and shoulders were entwined in an intricate crisscross of leather straps
and slings; several camera bags dangled from his neck. He dragged behind him an airport handcart piled high with portable lights and his
ninety-five-pound electric generator.

"Why are you talking like that?" he asked.

We fought our way out from the baggage claim section. Eager young
Texans in ten-gallon hats and snakeskin boots snatched their luggage

from the spinning carousel, and then hustled into the metropolitan blur that blends Dallas into Fort Worth.

"'Howdy,'" I explained, "is a southwestern colloquialism. *Howdy.* Meaning, 'How do you do?' Surely, even in Brooklyn, you heard people say 'Howdy.'"

"Yo," he said, "no way."

I should have explained to him that before arriving in Dallas earlier in the week, I had spent several evenings in front of my television at home watching the six-hour video encore presentation of *Lonesome Dove*, the country's latest favorite western epic. The movie had faithfully re-created Larry McMurtry's novel chronicling a handful of nineteenth-century misfits who slowly push their rustled herd up the Texas cattle trails to the grassy promised land of Montana. On the flight from San Francisco to Dallas everybody in the plane seemed to be reading something by McMurtry or Max Brand or Luke Short. As we sailed over the Rockies, above the torrid flatlands of Zane Grey's Arizona, and across the painted desert of Louis L'Amour's New Mexico, finally skidding down three hundred miles beyond the frontier marker of J. Frank Dobie's Pecos River, all two-hundred-and-thirty-five heads aboard the jetliner were bobbling along to the drawling pace of the western novel. Overnight everybody in America wanted once again to be a cowboy.

"The rental company didn't have any compacts or midsize cars," I informed Lonny, "so I upgraded us to something we won't be ashamed to drive around here. Something with horsepower." I also had been reading *Lonesome Dove.*

"These people," whispered Lonny, as we thrashed our way through the terminal toward the rental car counter, "they all think they're *cowboys!*" As a transplanted New Yorker now living in Berkeley, he couldn't begin to imagine why Texans thought that their state was a grand American place.

"You just need some grub," I coaxed. "You're probably dog-tired and mule-hungry."

"Stop this moronic nonsense."

"Or maybe it's vicey-versey."

"Immediately!"

Most of all, he seemed unnerved by the ten-gallon hats floating atop the airport's wild river of heads. In an age when most metropolitan airports assume the stunning sameness of suburban shopping malls, the Dallas–Fort Worth hub had managed to sustain the tangy flavor of its regional culture, even if the distinction relied upon caricature. Lonny insisted that it was like flying into Los Angeles International and discovering that everybody wore Mickey Mouse ears; he seemed to think that the entire state had dressed up that day for our benefit.

"Don't you get it, hoss?" I asked him. "We're in Texas now."

"Yes, but does everybody have to keep making such a big deal out of it?"

"I reckon they do."

"And don't call me 'hoss'. You're not one of them, so don't even pretend that you are. *Hoss.* My God!"

~~~~~

The American imagination was having trouble with Texas. From the other forty-nine states, the view focused upon the lonely streets of boomtown Houston gone bust, the recollection of Dallas as the City of Assassination, the quicksand of bankrupt S&Ls absorbing all residual petrodollars, the posse of politicians who, if not the nation's most craven, were certainly among its most shameless—basing their latest gubernatorial campaign upon the vexing question of which candidate, if elected, would dispatch the largest number of criminals to the electric chair with the greatest discernible glee. Contemporary Texas flew too many flags indicating the general dismaying drift of the entire nation. But mythical frontier Texas was staging a nick-of-time return.

For Lonny and me, this renewed enthusiasm for the cowboy culture posed a problem since we were unarguably city slickers.

Neither of us had ever saddled a horse, milked a cow, shot a rifle at something that might turn around to bite us if we missed, watched a John Wayne movie on purpose, or worn a cowboy hat without satiric intent. These omissions can be read upon visitors' faces like bad sunburns and provoke among Texans their notorious desiccated wit.

"Y'all from out of state?" asked the young fellow at the rent-a-car counter. Unsurprisingly, he wore a wide-brimmed Stetson, string tie, and blue jeans; his drawling voice echoed the honest and amiable curiosity of the wide-open plains. *Lonesome Dove*'s 945-page accumulation of cattlemen, Indians, gamblers, buffalo hunters, whores, sheriffs, and badmen had persuaded me that the state's mythic past must be forever imprinted even upon the frisky natives cantering across the Dallas–Fort Worth International Airport.

"Y'all never been to Texas before?" asked the counter clerk adamantly.

I studied these repetitious "y'alls." The term is a complex second-person-plural pronoun unknown outside the South except through mockery and inept imitation. For years, untutored city slickers across the country have been misappropriating the word, usually employing it in reference to an individual, as in, "Ma'am, y'all like to accompany me to the Public Theatre this Saturday night to see a new-fangled version of *Troilus and Cressida* set in Abilene?" In fact, the contraction is reserved for addressing two or more people: "Boys, y'all want to buy some of my vacant Houston high rises full of empty offices?"—thus implying fraternity, or at least, company. Texas is a big place and company is always noted.

"Where y'all going?" the young fellow asked.

"West," I answered in a tone that I thought might express the droll and rugged ethos of the frontier. "Between Odessa and Fort Davis."

"*Odessa?*" He laughed convulsively over this tremendous joke. His voice was as flat and dry as the prairie. "Why, that's the worst place on God's green earth. And *Fort Davis?* That's the most miserable, grace-foresaken devastation in our entire great state. Why you boys want to come all this way just to see a desert not fit for rattlesnakes?"

"Rattlesnakes?" echoed Lonny.

"Got 'em, though. And javelinas. You know, wild pigs. Little ones, though. Mean, though. Lots. Chase you boys up a tree. If there was a tree. But there ain't."

He tossed us the keys to our rented car and loosed the big fierce grin of his state. "Good luck, y'all."

Outside, we found our car in the company lot.

"What's that?" asked Lonny.

"That's our 1992 V-8, four-door, gas-guzzling Chrysler Imperial."

"Why?"

"So we can see the country, boy. Protect us against wild pigs. We could take refuge in there if we had to."

"We could raise a family of goats in there if we had to. Couldn't you get something less excessive?"

"It's a bargain. Since they didn't have the compact we reserved, we get this beauty at the same price. All we have to do is pay for the gas. I know what you're thinking, but they just don't drive Volvos around here. It's well known that Lee Harvey Oswald drove a Volvo."

Our 1992 V-8, four-door, gas-guzzling Chrysler Imperial was bright, blue, and humongous. It was a cow, a boat, a train, a veritable continent of a car: a rumbling monument to waste and excess. It reminded me of a friend's car I had coveted in high school—a '53 pearl-gray Plymouth, lowered to scrape the sidewalk, chopped and customized, boasting a useless tach and a red needle shaped like a devil's tail that spun 360 degrees around an archaic clockface speedometer whenever the driver stomped the pedal past forty mph. On Saturday evenings, we would rumble through Oakland's suburbs challenging strangers, offering to race for pink slips—and when we'd lose, as we must, somebody would dangle from the driver's seat window his sister's frilly pink negligee, laughing like a cretin as we chugged away.

Now twenty years later, our V-8, four-door, gas-guzzling Chrysler Imperial seemed the perfect vehicle in which to tour Texas for ten days. If a man can't ride a horse, he should at least be able to drive a Chrysler. Contemporary Texans, or anyway, the folks at the airport sporting the ten-gallon hats, who crowded the parking lot with monstrous four-door fuel pigs indistinguishable from our own rented car, all seemed to agree with this proposition. Together we might tear out to West Texas, draining six-packs of Lone Star and wasting far more than our fair share of fossil fuel.

I slipped into the driver's seat to face the confusion of one million dials adorning the dash like an airplane control panel. The Chrysler did not at all resemble the Chevy Nova that I drove back home.

"We'll hit the trail," I assured Lonny, "just as soon as I master these devices."

"Why are the windshield wipers going?"

"I thought they were the headlights."

"How come you opened the trunk?"

"Well, I reckon that's not the button for the rear defroster, is it?"

As soon as we located the highway, I noticed that the speedometer was screwy.

"Even if I step on the gas, nothing happens. The crazy thing just keeps flashing these numbers back at me that have nothing to do with how fast we're really going."

Lonny extracted the driver's manual from the glove compartment and studied it for ten minutes.

"That's because it's not the speedometer," he finally surmised, "it's the digital clock."

~~~~~~

One of the great pleasures of reading cowboy fiction is spending so much time with ordinary men and women (though Lord knows, it's mainly men) who have been cast upon a heroic landscape. By the conclusion of any respectable western yarn, these ordinary people end up heroes themselves. This plot line makes sense because anybody who could have survived a typical journey along the major cattle trails—running anywhere from the southern tip of Texas up through Indian Territory (Oklahoma) and on to Kansas, Nebraska, Wyoming, and Montana—seems otherwise fortified for all of life's future trials. By definition, mythic cowboys are much stronger, if not wiser, than the more reasonable folks back home who will wait and see how Manifest Destiny is turning out.

And there is little wonder that lots of folks did stay home. Despite the inner resources that a man or woman may bring to a heroic landscape, it can still kill you in fifty different ways. Cowboy fiction, from the preposterous dime novels of the 1860s to Larry McMurtry's elegiac and ironic westerns of today, come replete with trials of weather and circumstance that most of us would consider personal catastrophes if we had to live through them: dust storms, sleet storms, freezing rivers that must be forded day or night, even plagues of grasshoppers chirping madly like a living blanket of inexhaustible appetite and covering the plains, the cows, your own ten-gallon hat. On a heroic landscape, the sky blackens to slate in an instant, and the shallowest streams can be nested with water moccasins. Travel on a heroic landscape is a gruesome adventure.

Lonny and I had been traveling throughout the country on our own gruesome adventure. We were collaborating on a series of magazine articles about the chemical contamination of the nation's small towns and rural communities, which prompted an exhaustive itinerary of hazardous waste hotspots we'd come to think of as our North American Toxic Tour. Neither of us had seen Texas before, but we'd discussed earlier the necessity of getting a look at the state, if only to distinguish it from the more ghastly places we'd been recently visiting.

In the past twelve months, we'd toured the chromium slag heaps of New Jersey, the petrochemical swill of Louisiana's bayous, the poisonous overflow bubbling up from the abandoned lead, zinc, and copper mines of rural Oklahoma, the eye-stinging industrial skylines of places like Nitro, West Virginia. The month before, we'd spent two awful weeks in Ohio, visiting an array of hazardous waste incinerators and conversing with some edgy people who lived on the perimeter of a 750,000-metric-ton toxic dump. Occasionally, one of the neighborhood's abandoned homes would explode from the methane venting up through the landfill.

We had expected from Ohio the usual unsightly spectacles of sludge, muck, and postindustrial devastation, but what we hadn't been prepared for was the intense dullness of the scenery. At its best, Ohio boils down to one bright red barn, with a whitewashed picket fence, thrust amid an endless roll of feeble hills and abject weediness. The flavor of the landscape is vanilla, its dominant color milky-gray, its sounds the bucolic hum of crickets and Muzak. Each night after work, we'd retreat to our Comfort Inn to read aloud another doleful story from Sherwood Anderson's *Winesburg, Ohio*, noting the celebrated spiritual void that

was deftly served by the objective correlative of the scenic emptiness
we experienced each day along the road. Even our AAA map betrayed
us, pinpointing with a broken green line the supposedly scenic route
we drove 150 miles out of our way to follow, which turned out to be
the cluttered path of industrial decline, from Cleveland to Sandusky—
dirty, dying red-brick towns set against the flat gray waters of the lifeless
Great Lakes. We knew then that we had to find another way to continue
our work that wouldn't turn us forever against the landscapes of our
own country.

Our plan was to bathe ourselves in the regional myths, accept everything, and sink deeply, if temporarily, into whatever the territory had to
offer. It was not clear that Ohio had anything at all to offer, but Texas
prided itself on offering more than anybody needed of everything. Texas
was cowboys. And the cowboy, more than any other relic of American
popular culture, was accessible to us in books, both great and ghastly.

In fact, the Western divides perfectly into two traditions: the literary
novels of lasting reputation (beginning with James Fenimore Cooper's
Leatherstocking Tales, which nobody would read today except under
the threat of being dragged down the street by four horses), and the
long line of popular sagas characterized now by Louis L'Amour and his
brethren, which earn the unanimous indifference of critics everywhere
and sell millions of copies around the world.

Both traditions bear an interesting lineage.

After Cooper, the literary Western owes almost everything to Owen
Wister's 1902 novel, *The Virginian*. Wister basically invented the cowboy epic, with its Galahad from the East roving West to prove his man-
hood on the playing fields of the frontier. This mythical formulation
paralleled Wister's own experience. He had studied music at Harvard,
where he was enthralled by Wagnerian opera. In 1885, Wister drifted
onto a Wyoming ranch to seek a rest cure for his neuralgia and depres-

sion. From this unlikely confluence of cows and Wagner, he created the nameless knight of the prairies whose literary and cinematic descendants have yet to stop reproducing. (In the book's second chapter, the Virginian utters the most famous of all Western imperatives: "When you say that, *smile.*") The book proved an immediate success, selling three hundred thousand copies in two years and well over a million copies by 1920. In this tradition, there followed a host of capable writers like Zane Grey (a former dentist from Manhattan, whose eighty-five books sold thirteen million copies during his lifetime), as well as a far less distinguished string of imitators who held close to the established myth, recasting it over the years in iron.

The popular Western, on the other hand, owes less to Wagner than to the cheap thrills of incessant horseplay and violence transpiring upon a landscape of moral righteousness. This is the frontier of white hats versus black hats, culled from the newspaper-inflated exploits of historical figures such as Kit Carson and Jim Bridger (whose vocation as fur traders actually made them far more familiar with beavers than cows). This tradition of exaggeration assumed its full-blown fictional guise in Erastus Beadle's dime novel series, which appeared in the 1860s. Beadle's books weren't really novels, since they only ran about thirty thousand words and were ground out by iron-seated scribes in New York at the incredible rate of one thousand words per hour over twelve-hour shifts; but they did cost a dime and, therefore, found a huge audience with initial print runs reaching sixty thousand copies. Easterners absorbed everything they could read about the West, even if it was being written by their next-door neighbors, thus changing forever America's self-image. "The Frontier has become conscious of itself, acts the part for the Eastern visitor," complained Frank Norris (the author of *The Octopus* and *McTeague*) in 1890, "and this self-consciousness is a sign, surer than all others, of the decadence of a type, the passing of an epoch."

~~~~~~

Later that night, after we figured out how to unlock the gas tank and fuel up the Chrysler, Lonny and I dropped off the camera equipment at the Best Western and journeyed out to search for the real West. We'd been inspired to invest an evening in Fort Worth (or Cow Town as the city is legendarily known throughout Texas) because of a conversation that I'd had back in Dallas the day before. I'd been speaking with three lifelong Lone Star Staters who divulged that they'd never actually been to Fort Worth, even though it stood only thirty minutes away on the interstate, its miniature skyline etched into the horizon from the vantage of Dallas's suburbs.

"Fort Worth?" drawled one belle, incredulously. "That's like going to the real Texas!"

The spot Lonny and I landed for the evening was Billy Bob's Texas, "the world's largest indoor honky-tonk," a famously oversized cowboy saloon, sprawling across nearly one hundred thousand square feet, equipped with forty-two bar stations and two rambling dance floors. From the talk I'd heard in Dallas, I'd anticipated some great atavistic drunken roughhouse—more like a Northern California biker bar, filled with colorful sociopaths quick to interpret any glance, nod, gesture, or unfamiliar regional accent as a challenge to Texas itself (Remember the Alamo!), and then the glass would shatter and furniture would start flying. This was the kind of scene that occurred quite regularly in Beadle's dime novels, such as *Roaring Ralph Rockwood*, *The Reckless Ranger* and *Deadwood Dick's Claim; Or, The Fairy Face of Faro Flats*.

In truth, Billy Bob's is a peaceful place. Rather than being cast deep in the heart of Texas, the place seemed like Fisherman's Wharf with cowboys.

But the real reason I dragged Lonny to Billy Bob's was to see the bulls. On weekends, Billy Bob's Texas operates an indoor bull-riding ring.

We paid our two dollars and climbed into the bleachers, surrounded by highway-sized billboards advertising Copenhagen snuff and Skoal chewing tobacco. I was primed to admire the amateur rodeo riders and applaud like crazy. Lonny perused the book review section of the *New York Times*.

"Pay attention now," I told him, as the first bull and rider dashed out from the gate.

Above the bull ring, the bulbous-nosed rodeo announcer flagged his Stetson at the crowd and whooped into the public address system. "How do you freeze a woman from the waist down?" he cackled, killing time until the fallen rider could scamper back to safety after clinging to an angry fellow named Earl for a remarkable six seconds.

"Is it over now?" asked Lonny.

"*Marry her!*"

The judges loitered upon a parapeted walkway suspended above the bull ring, muttering into one another's faces about the young man's sudden discombobulation. The bleachers crowd was composed of courting couples clad in androgynous sharp-pressed blue jeans, plus legions of drunken, dateless young men wearing regulation pearl-button, long-sleeve shirts and the inevitable Stetsons. The courageous and perhaps insane young bull riders, also in their early twenties, wore denim jackets with the trade name *Wrangler* embroidered in a white crescent across their backs.

"What does Eye-Rack and Hee-Row-She-Ma got in common?" demanded the giddy announcer as another young rider hit the dust and then clambered over the rail fence to safety.

Lonny pointed to an advertisement in the *Times* noting that the new biography of Wittgenstein had been issued in paperback.

"*Nothing. Yet. . . .*"

We must have watched for a half-hour. Finally, I was forced to conclude that the bulls and the boys did not indicate the true heart of Texas today—and even less the Texas of 120 years past that I'd been reading about in Wister, Grey, McMurtry, and all the rest. The spectacle more closely resembled a county fair curiosity, like a two-headed calf or a singing rooster. Its chief attraction was the anomalous thrill of a bull running riot indoors. Of course, working cowboys still exist, though mainly in the Texas hinterlands. But their impersonators outnumber them vastly. To most people living in Dallas, Houston, San Antonio— even Fort Worth—working cowboys are like singing roosters, remarkable but beside the point.

To find the true heart of Texas, we'd have to ride into the countryside and delve more deeply into our books.

"What did you think about the bulls?" I asked Lonny. Our rented blue boat of a Chrysler sped down Highway 35 South toward Waco.

"I didn't think anything about them and neither did you. In fact, I didn't notice anybody thinking much about anything in that place, or else they wouldn't have been riding on top of those wild animals."

"I thought they weren't very persuasive bulls."

Waco flashed past us in a speckled blur.

"You've been here in Texas three days longer than me and now you're some kind of expert on the personalities of livestock?"

"I liked the one named Earl. He had persuasive horns."

"Drive," said Lonny, "and remember that you don't know the first thing about it."

We drove all morning until we reached Johnson City, birthplace of the former president, now a state park. At the ranger's station, Lonny purchased a tape titled *The Wit of LBJ* for the Chrysler's cassette deck. The tape was stuffed with sundry quips averaging about twelve seconds, each indebted to the jaunty public speaking style of Rotary Club luncheons. ("I am reminded of a story told to me by the Postmaster

General," drawled the ex-president.) But *The Wit of LBJ* cannot be listened to twice over, and soon we were enjoying the soundtrack to *Urban Cowboy.*

"Where'd you get that tape?"

"Back at the gas station. I bought it when you were in the bathroom."

"The gas station with the flag of the Lone Star State hanging over the urinals?"

"No, the one with the picture of Willie Nelson pasted to the back of the cash register."

We veered west, ambling through the hill country. I slowed down for some cattle wandering across the road.

"You know," said Lonny, "he's really from Brooklyn."

"You're mad! There isn't anybody in the world more Texan than Willie Nelson."

"No, John Travolta. *He's* from Brooklyn. He starred in *Urban Cowboy* with Debra Winger. I saw it once on an airplane. That's basically all I know about Texas. That and what those stupid books you've been reading out loud every night are supposed to tell us."

The thunderstorm broke outside of Dripping Springs. Rain washed down upon the Chrysler's windshield like a waterfall. I'm tempted to say that the noise resembled a TNT explosion, which sounds appropriately Texan with its intimations of oil rig mishaps and avalanches in the Davis Mountains. In truth, I know what explosives sound like from a near distance because as a kid I lived down the street from a gunpowder factory. Several times every year, the powder works would blow up, sending us scurrying beneath our school desks in preparation for what Texas hill-country thunder does scarily suggest: the opening strains of nuclear war. In reality, TNT simply *pops,* a single boom. Texas hill-country thunder announces itself with that same single pop; then it mushrooms, fizzling and blaring with an alarming swell until it cracks like the world's largest tree limb, and you expect the entire sky to light up with the incandescence of Armageddon.

Texas thunder sounds *risky*, which is what Texans like to intimate about their state in general. When Lonny and I pulled into Wimberly, a small town outside of Austin, we soon stumbled upon another example of how the state commemorates its dangers.

While dining at the Dairy Queen, we noticed a prominent wall poster touting the local high-school football team. The poster featured the team photo, with block letters gathered underneath proclaiming, WHEN THE DUST HAS CLEARED, THE TEXANS WILL BE ON TOP. One wit had modified the lettering on his uniform jersey to read *The Texins*, which I interpreted as a satiric poke at the notorious no pass/no play rule, pushed through the Texas state legislature by the widely resented educational reformer, H. Ross Perot. The Texas billionaire insisted that students should learn how to spell and the like before they trod upon the playing field. Many of his fellow Lone Star Staters disagreed.

But it was the guns that threw us. In the portrait, each snarling teenager cradled a deer rifle or shotgun. One kid toted a large, handsome pistol with its wobbly barrel dangling in the air like a hickory switch. The guns weren't actually pointed at anybody. But they seemed ready enough.

I knew from reading *Riders of the Purple Sage* that weapons had always been sacred in this part of the country. ("Gun-packing in the West since the Civil War," asserts Lassiter, the novel's fast-draw hero, "has growed into a kind of moral law.") But back home in Oakland, this football team portrait would never play since the guns would be regarded not as symbols but real weapons. The Wimberly kids inhabited no less a mythical world than their cowboy models. At the edge of town, the kids could fire off a few rounds into the air and never worry about bullets raining down upon a crowd of bystanders. They could luxuriate in violence without consequences amid the countryside's splendid isolation, telling themselves that Texans were peaceable people at heart, though nobody should mess with them. Of course, this was the message that Zane Grey and Max Brand had popularized about Texas from their homes in New York and Hollywood. But for anybody actually traveling across the state (I was now halfway through reading *Lonesome Dove*), the real story was more complicated.

People who rate Texas poorly often turn out to have driven across it in a single burst of droning energy. This kind of recklessness, coupled with the region's relentless prairies and plains, results in the state's bad reputation and inaccurate characterization as a wasteland. Only part of Texas is a wasteland. Admittedly, it's a big part, spacious enough to accommodate entire nations the size of Mauritania or the Spanish Sahara, which this portion of the state's sudden and startling blankness somewhat resembles.

The source of most outsiders' consternation is the *Llano Estacado*, or the staked plain, that flat, dry extension of the Midwest's Great Plains that droops down from the Panhandle to smother all life and hope from Highway 40 around Amarillo to Big Spring and Odessa in the southwest, and then dribbles down to the Edwards Plateau. Yet it's the *Llano Estacado* that affords visitors the opportunity to squarely face the realm and reason of Texas's famed frontier values.

The first frontier value that Lonny and I had to confront coalesced around the most basic aspects of manual dexterity: could we actually manage, like men, to drive the Chrysler without some lethal confusion regarding its many dials and gauges that would result in our beetling off the miserably marked highway and skidding into a quicksand bog or the only tree standing within two hundred miles? After driving for a couple of days, I felt that the car was finally under acceptable control, even though the Chrylser's headlights kept popping back on after we'd turned them off, and all we had to worry about now was getting lost, which was, in fact, a constant concern.

Lonny carried a small compass chained to his belt. This device might seem like ample protection against our collective sense of misdirection, but somehow it was not. Over the past few months, we had so often found ourselves totally lost after the conclusion of a lengthy interview in some tiny toxic hotspot that we now budgeted extra hours simply to wander around in dogged confusion while searching for the right road out of town. Bigger cities naturally presented bigger problems. Leaving Austin, we'd doubled back four times on the same highway, unable to reconcile the evidence of the compass, road map, and our own fallible instincts. After wasting nearly three hours trying to launch ourselves further westwards, we finally gave up and headed for the nearest Motel-6 offering free access to a classic movie station, which that night broadcast *The Ox-Bow Incident*, one of the most literary Westerns, written by Walter van Tilburg Clark.

The hard truth was that, in regards to pathfinding, the two of us added up to the exact opposite of Joshua Deets, whom I had been reading about in *Lonesome Dove*. Deets could negotiate the true course at all times in any weather, even in a "country that seemed to contain nothing except itself." I admired Deets. I envied him. And I knew that the closest I would ever get to somebody like him was in the pages of McMurtry's novel.

Texas's expansiveness also impressed upon me another masculine imperative: Lonny and I had to stop whining every time we got lost, since getting lost was bound to happen.

A policy of reduced whining makes sense in Texas. From its earliest days, Texas has demanded the full store of clenched-jaw stoicism. And if you must say something, clip it short. This is the primary aesthetic of Texas conversation, reflected in the scraped-scruff nature of the land-

scape. When we pulled over for breakfast at a small cafe in Balmorhea—
a dusty little spot off the highway that could be any one of one thousand
unlovable little towns—I eavesdropped on a conversation that stuck in
my memory for months, if only for its artful circularity and restraint.

"Wasn't ol' Jerry 'bout sixty when he died?" asked one of four hulky
men in their late fifties who sat around the cafe's large breakfast table.
They were dawdling over their morning coffee with the patience of liz-
ards whose biggest effort of the day would be sunning themselves on
hot rocks.

"Seemed like he just got his Social Security."

"Then what happened to that ol' dog of his?"

"I believe somebody stole that dog."

"Them dogs can be worth some money."

"I got an old dog in my backyard. I get along with him just fine."

"Ever see a mongoose kill a cobra?"

"I seen that on television. Planning to get me one of them satellite
dishes."

"Give you cancer."

"Ol' Jerry just bought one of them satellite dishes with his Social
Security."

"I just might get me another ol' dog."

The best Texas talk chases its own tail in comical slow motion. Masters of indirection and genuises of inflection, Texans leave plenty of room
between every phrase from which to puzzle out a vast plain of possible
meanings.

"A lyricism appropriate to the Southwest needs to be as clean as
a bleached bone and as well-spaced as trees on the Llano," Larry
McMurtry once wrote, invoking the virtues of his own best books. "The
elements still dominate here, and a spare, elemental language, with now
and then a touch of elegance, will suffice. We could probably use Mark

Twain, but I doubt we're yet civilized enough to need a Henry James."

Rolling across the plains, I felt no curiosity whatsoever about what Henry James might have had to say about all this emptiness. But I did sense the inevitable throb toward storytelling as a pastime to which all human beings will resort when faced with unrelieved travel.

"You know that story I told you back there about three hundred miles ago?" I asked Lonny, after we'd been driving all morning. "The one about how when we were kids, my sister and I always wanted a horse?"

"No," said Lonny, staring out the window at nothing.

"Sure, you do. And how our parents told us they couldn't afford it, that there wasn't room for a horse in the suburbs, and we wouldn't be able to take care of a horse anyway since we were only about seven or eight years old—and so we should just forget the whole thing until we grew up, and then we could move to Texas or Montana or Wyoming and become cowpersons? Of course, they didn't use that word."

"Nope, don't remember."

"But my sister and I kept whining and complaining and driving everybody crazy until one afternoon our dad brought us over to our uncle's house who'd just found one of those big, grey, smooth dogs wandering around his street. You know, those dogs that are so stupid they forget how to wag their tails. What do you call them? Weimaraners! And he told us that the weimaraner was a horse?"

"No, I guess I wasn't listening."

"And our dad said that if we could teach him to graze in our backyard then we could keep him and ride him bareback?"

"I have no recollection of this story."

"And so we brought the weimaraner home, and tried and tried, but the stupid thing wouldn't eat the grass, and we got really worried that our dad was going to give our horse—the weimaraner, you understand—back to our uncle. And so one day, after we came home from school, before either of our parents got back from work, we yanked up all the yellow and purple chrysanthemums that Mom had planted in her flower-boxes, tossed them over the fence into the neighbor's yard, and told our parents the great news that our horse was finally grazing out back, but he liked flowers best."

"No!"

"Well, anyway," I said, "I made that story up. Didn't you think it was just a little bit *improbable*? Anyway, you should have realized that I made it up because *you know* that I don't even have a sister. I made it all up just to pass the time."

"That's fine with me. I didn't even notice that you were talking."

He flicked on the car radio.

"Well, then I guess I don't have to worry about boring you when I repeat the same story three hours from now."

Lonny spun the radio dial, and we listened to the country stations' identical sad-ass stories: songs that spelled out all the variations of lost love and faded love, betrayal and crazy vengeance, steadfast loyalty and low-down meanness. There were cheating songs, leaving songs, songs about trucks and trains and prison that pretend not to be really about cheating, leaving, and losing—every conceivable version of the lovesick blues from casual regrets to slipping under the porch like a sick hog and wishing to die. All that stuff you get to thinking about far from home while traveling on a road as hard as a fist with its big arm stretched out to eternity.

"I hope they play that Waylon Jennings song again," I said, staring straight ahead through the dust-dappled windshield at nothing what-soever.

"Which Waylon Jennings song?"

"The one about him leaving somebody for somebody else."

"They're all about somebody leaving somebody for somebody else."

"Or getting left," I pointed out.
Fifteen minutes passed. Or maybe three hours.
"How many more miles to Odessa?"
"Look at the map."
He did.
"About a million."

~~~~~~

In much of the Southwest's regional literature, people are constantly complaining, with or without the requisite Texas reserve, about how damn lonely they feel. The never-ending trail's insistent lonesome cry echoes through the collected works of Zane Grey, J. Frank Dobie, Louis L'Amour. And most affectingly, it rebounds between the pages of Larry McMurtry's novels. Lonesome sits squarely in the title of McMurtry's best book. It suffuses the speech and thoughts of his most likable characters as far back as *The Last Picture Show*, McMurtry's youthful elegy to growing up rough and tender in West Texas. And it has everything to do with the landscape.

Texas may be the country's best state in which to be lonesome.

Of course, West Texas isn't desolate in the manner of New York or Los Angeles; it's just the opposite. All that unbroken countryside breeds a yearning for other people. So instead of sifting through the urban throng for a familiar face (or, more likely, avoiding the gaze of strangers), you'll take any face at all. At least, it's a human face, which explains why leathernecked Texans rambling across their network of backroads and detours in their rusted pick-up trucks and ferocious four-by-fours wave so gallantly to every other car sporting Texas plates.

All this lonesomeness is another reason McMurtry's Texas epics feel so familiar and appealing. McMurtry renders unwanted solitude into a physical malady; you can feel the loneliness like a gut ache or sore knees. His cowboys aren't singing roosters; they throb with the same quiet heartache that we experience when seated around a sad campfire or listening to the tireless grasp of the ocean or gazing up at the Texas prairie's bright, unsullied blanket of stars. As McMurtry has admitted, "the place where all my stories start is the heart faced suddenly with the loss of its country, its customary and legendary range."

In the hands of lesser writers, this longing for the past might boil down to phony sentiment for a past that never existed—the sanitized West, the West minus the tedium, cholera, genocide. But McMurtry's vision of the frontier rings true without diminishing its heroic scale because he's willing to accommodate the mythic past to our ironic present: his characters feel as lonely as we do sailing across those same daunting plains and prairies, though of course we're insulated from hardship by air-conditioning and cassette decks.

Everybody's lonesome because there's no further road to travel.

"Men are free when they belong to a living, organic, *believing* community," wrote D. H. Lawrence of the American frontier, "active in fulfilling some unfulfilled, perhaps unrealized purpose. . . . The most unfree souls go west, and shout of freedom. Men are freest when they are most unconscious of freedom. The shout is a rattling of chains, always was."

McMurtry's nineteenth-century lawmen, sod-breakers, and ranchers' wives agree with Lawrence. They have run out of frontier and they know it. Yet we modern Americans, including Texans, and especially the Texans in McMurtry's most lonesome novels about modern America, such as *Moving On* and *Texasville*, long ago reached the frontier's indisputable end—and won't admit it.

"I still want to see a javelina," Lonny admitted, as we drove out of Fort Davis. Our work was completed, and we were exhausted from nearly two weeks on the road—and maybe just a little tired of each other too.

"Look!" I cried. "A javelina!"

"No, that's a dog."

"You sure?"

"It's wearing a collar."

"But it's spotted!" I thumped the cover to the Texas guidebook that I'd purchased somewhere along the road. "It says here that javelinas can be spotted."

"That barking thing with the long tail chasing the cat out of the fire station is a dalmatian. I thought you had some experience with dogs?"

"I thought you weren't listening to my stories?"

"I thought you might finally say something worth listening to," he reasoned, "but I can see you haven't."

Two weeks on the road with anybody can be rough. If this kind of conversation is as bad as it gets, then you know you're good friends. I'll never understand how those lonesome cowboys survived six months on the trail with no recess from one another's same old stories.

I dipped back into my guidebook while Lonny drove.

"Did you know that javelinas are not wild pigs," I asked him, "but rather members of an extremely small family of mammals called Tayassuidae? It says so here in chapter two."

"Tell me more." At least it was something new to jaw over.

"Javelinas are more closely related to tapirs and horses than pigs. And according to page 118, the typical javelina is well-mannered, nearsighted, and nothing to fear."

"For us," pointed out Lonny, "that's a good thing."

Of course, he was right. By now, it was all too obvious that Lonny and I did not collectively nor individually possess the traditional Texan virtues that had culled the state from the frontier and might have proved helpful had we been faced with a genuinely feral and furious pig.

But then, why should we?

Despite the exhortations of the books and landscapes against which we had measured ourselves and come up short, Lonny and I weren't really drifters on the lonesome prairie compelled to survive by our wits; no more than the kids at Billy Bob's were rodeo stars, or the Wimberly High School football team was a pack of gunslingers, or the people at the airport were Lone Star State pioneers.

Everybody might like to have sprung from the true heart of Texas. But where, if not in books, was this legendary place located?

Could the true heart of Texas be found amid the scrubby flatlands of Midland-Odessa, where W. P. Webb's Rangers patrolled the border? Or was Texas really the basin and range province of the Trans-Pecos, nostalgically adorned with classic southwestern Zane Grey purple sage? Was J. Frank Dobie's Llano Uplift (a huge white limestone and pink granite prehistoric bump rising up from the middle of the state) more genuinely Texan than the overgrazed cattle region along the Rio Grande Plain with its subtropical brush and bramble—the cactus, mesquite, yucca, and huajillo forming the high plains chaparral of countless dime novels? Was the Hill Country or the East Texas Forests or the Gulf Coast described by Roy Bedichek (and Max Brand and Luke Short) more evocatively, legendarily Texas than any other part of the state? Partisans of every region will claim that they inhabit the true heart of Texas; but, of course, the true Texas is as multifarious as the true United States of America, which may be why some xenophobic Texans assert that their state is basically the nation itself, but more so.

Finally, despite all appearances (and many people's experience) Texas today is fundamentally an urban state, part of the modern world, an inescapable place. Forget the pull of the plains, the romance of the prairies; forget about being a cowboy. Most Texans today live in cities. Texas is Houston; it's Dallas and San Antonio, Corpus Christi and Brownsville.

The notion that we're still a country of cowboys is one of our nation's most extravagant illusions. But that's also one of the truly grand things about Texas: despite the intrusion of everyday reality, it's still a big enough place to let our imaginations roam. There is still room for the romantic daydreams spurred on by listening to stories and reading books. And in this wandering, we might become—if only for a moment—what we know we can never really be.

Off Highway 20, leaving Odessa, Lonny and I pulled to the side for our last Texas dinner in one more nameless cafe. We ordered a couple of beers and two chicken-fried steaks. ("Only a rank degenerate would drive 1,500 miles across Texas," McMurtry once wrote, "without eating a chicken-fried steak.")

In the other room, off the lunch counter, the jukebox blared the Waylon Jennings tune that I had longed to hear earlier in the week. Somebody else with a fistful of quarters must have felt the same way because the jukebox played the song five times over until its plug was yanked from the wall socket and Waylon wound down to a scratchy wheeze. Above the jukebox's final strains, I could make out the unmistakable twang of live country music tuning up inside the bar.

The small, smoky bar was the size of a half-dozen pool tables, but it managed to accommodate about thirty couples, ranging from their late teens up into their early sixties. Where they'd all come from I couldn't imagine; there had only been a couple of pick-up trucks parked out front. Most of the men wore black or cream-colored Stetsons, though they probably weren't really cowboys. They must have been truck drivers, teachers, welders, grocery clerks. They did all the unromantic, necessary work that small towns offer, work that has nothing to do with punching cows. Their ladies were dressed in hand-embroidered blouses and tight-pressed blue jeans that outlined the curve of their thighs like the slopes of lacquered hills. They stood hand-in-hand, their sunburnt faces squinting in the darkness up toward the stage, their jaws stubbornly set to squeeze a few good hours out of Saturday night.

I ordered another Lone Star long-neck and wandered across the room to watch the dancing. The most graceful couples—and there were many —glided across the floor with supple dignity. On stage, the country-and-western band, consisting of an electric guitar, stand-up bass, rhythm guitar, and drums, played "The Silver-Tongued Devil" by Kris Kristofferson and then a string of old Willie Nelson hits. Lonny took a seat at the bar, tapping his foot in rhythm to the heavy pounding of the bass drum.

Then the band launched into "You Never Even Call Me by My Name," a send-up of country music, written by Chicagoan city slicker Steve Goodman, but better known among C&W fans for its interpretation by the jailbird-and-country-music outlaw, David Allan Coe. I've always admired this song, its message being that the "perfect" country song must contain references to trucks, trains, Mama, getting drunk, going to prison, and several other themes now regarded by most aficionados to be the essence of the genre. It was a great joke on all those people throughout the country who thought they were cowboys, but weren't; and all the people tonight in the nameless little cafe outside of Odessa, Texas, who weren't cowboys any more than I was, seemed to know all the words.

As the couples formed a huge wagon wheel, promenading side-by-side, pivoting and then twirling, spinning and sidestepping around one another until they faced the outside of the circle, I could read upon the lips of practically every man and woman under fifty the identical tattoo of the lip-synched song. They'd memorized the lyrics like a prayer, down to every grunt and whisper, the affectionate echo of explicit parody.

When the drummer clashed his cymbals eight times in conclusion, I faced the stage and stared at the band's name plastered in six-inch, red-sequined letters across the head of the bass drum: THE HEARTS OF TEXAS. As the next tune began—it was Tammy Wynette's "D-I-V-O-R-C-E"—many of the couples kissed and embraced or groped for one another's hands in the darkness, and then they strolled back across the floor toward the dim, smoky light of the bar.

UNDERNEATH
WILLA CATHER'S NEBRASKA

There was nothing but land, not a country at all,

but the materials out of which countries are made.

—Willa Cather, *My Ántonia*

Scotts Bluff towers eight hundred feet above the North Platte Valley floor, providing a firm, flat table upon which to view the country. Atop the headland's steep summit, Ann and I gasped for breath, massaged our quadriceps, and clapped our arms around each other's waists to stand at the cliff's edge and silently admire what I had feared: nothing and nothing and nothing, as far as we both could see.

Throughout the spring, Ann and I had been debating the wisdom of planning a trip back to Nebraska in July. Ann wanted to visit her hometown during the hottest, dullest, flattest month of the year. Atop the bluff, everything we now saw, or didn't see, confused rather than confirmed my misgivings. Nebraska was certainly a flat, empty place. But there was nothing dull about the scenery.

"Nebraska can surprise you," Ann had warned back in California. "Most people don't appreciate the place. Sometimes *I* don't appreciate it."

Like many foolish partisans of either coast, I had long presumed that Nebraska was an unsuitable site for an agreeable visit. I envisioned a big, stolid hay bale of a place, composed largely of perfect right angles, with one ragged edge flagging the corn belt. I thought of Nebraska as the epitome of those crafty states whose indeterminate location in the center of an unmarked map confounds the majority of our nation's young geography students.

Nebraska, the misperceived and misplaced.

In the midst of our argument, Ann shimmered off to the bookshelf. She returned with a well-thumbed paperback edition of *My Ántonia*, Willa Cather's novel about the immigrant Scandinavians, Germans, French, and Bohemians who settled southeastern Nebraska's farm country in the late nineteenth century. Over the years, Willa Cather has provided Ann with persuasive evidence that her home state has been largely maligned and misunderstood by the rest of us. She told me to read the book. And that's how we now found ourselves wiping the sweat from our faces atop Scotts Bluff while admiring the infamous emptiness.

Nebraska is best perceived from this height. On top of the bluff, everything below seems even flatter, more severe, endless. This view mirrors the terrible sameness that assailed the first settlers moving west. For every drugstore clerk and cobbler's wife departing from St. Joseph, Missouri, with an overfilled twelve-foot Conestoga wagon and some appreciation for life's constant struggle, the western Nebraska plains—deemed, no less, the Great American Desert—must have looked like the bottom of the world.

Historians of the westward migration maintain that the plains drove some people crazy; it was so boring. Scotts Bluff was a blessed change, rising up in swift relief to the infernal flatness. Not as exciting as the feared but infrequent war parties of Cheyenne and Sioux, but dramatic enough; and as welcome a diversion as might be found along the trail until Denver.

But the far end of Nebraska, though impressive in its vacancy, is still the rocky West, not the blazing middle of the nation; it isn't Willa Cather territory. And it was the middle of the state that had weighted Ann's argument in favor of spending several weeks there. So when we climbed down from the bluff, we stepped into our borrowed car and pointed ourselves toward the heartland.

Scores of miles blurred into hundreds. We caught roadside glimpses of Lewellen, Gothenburg, and the North Platte River. By the time we hit the middle of the state, where Nebraskan farmland fits squarely into the shoulders of Iowa and Kansas, leaving behind the West to form that troika of ordinariness known as Middle America, Ann said that she felt in her bones once again that Nebraska could be the perfect place in which to grow up. And she told me the following story.

One summer afternoon, when she was a little girl visiting her grandparents in Beaver City, Nebraska (population 780), Ann slipped up to the attic to prowl around for hidden treasures. While she hadn't been expressly forbidden to explore the attic alone, she had been warned often enough about touching things that didn't belong to her. Nothing inside the attic belonged to her, but she furtively probed and peeked and quietly ransacked every closet, trunk, and cupboard until she had to conclude that the dark attic smelled provocatively of the mysterious past (it was damp and musky, like a decaying cardboard box) but it truly held no treasures.

Then in a corner, she stumbled upon a great wrangle of plastic sheeting wound around a bundle of white lace. When she peeled back the plastic, its hardened layers crackled noisily and then cracked open like sun-split furrows in the summer garden. Ann heard footsteps on the stairs; spinning around on the heels of her bare feet, she suddenly faced her grandmother. "That's my wedding dress," her grandmother declared, arms folded across her chest. But she wasn't angry. In a moment, they were huddled together, unraveling the dress from its plastic layers. The woman hugged the wedding gown up against her chest, her exaggerated hips budding from either side, and then she pinned it against Ann's shoulders and beamed.

Ann said that for years, she fancied her grandmother must have been thinking about passing the dress down to her someday for her own wedding; she'd never seen her looking so dreamy. But by the time Ann grew old enough to wear the dress, it proved an impossible fit. At eighteen, Ann stood six feet tall, while her grandmother's head bobbed barely up to her shoulders. Nobody ever wore the dress again.

Now when Ann thinks back on that summer afternoon when they unwound the delicate lace and let it flutter to the floor, she realizes that her grandmother probably had not been daydreaming at all about some child's future wedding; she'd been reliving her own. Much of Nebraska, Ann insisted, was like the dress resurrected in the dim attic light: some dream of passion stored away for decades, only now and then privately revived.

As we drove south through the barbed whiskers of wheat and corn, I began to grasp what she meant. It was certainly possible to write off the countryside as an interminable plain. ("The only thing very noticeable about Nebraska," admonished Willa Cather's worried narrator in the opening pages of *My Ántonia*, "was that it was still, all day, Nebraska.") But by the time we'd reached the middle of the state, the dead sea of flat, sprawling land had lapped up upon itself in foamy waves of bristling alfalfa and sugar beets to form one of the most gorgeous landscapes I'd ever seen.

Now perhaps it's just the contrariness of human imagination, but all this land sewn together in ample, undulating strips inevitably suggests its opposite to the scanning eye. In the language of the Omaha Indians, Nebraska means "flat water." And today people still talk persistently about the land in terms better suited to oceans, lakes, and rivers—probably because there isn't much real water around. Except for the Platte River, Nebraska is a dry place, renowned among the early pioneers for its nonexistent streams and ponds coruscating across the plains in maddening mirage. But once the plains break midstate, the shaggy grain fields wag and ripple in the breezes like an ocean about to rise up from its calm, and it's here that you make a discovery that's as startling as the first geographer's revelation about the roundness of the Earth: Nebraska isn't all flat. In fact, much of the hilly grassland streaming through the state's side roads and detours bucks and rolls so insistently as to almost make you seasick. Cather wrote that "the grass was the country, as the water is the sea. The red of the grass made all the great prairie the colour of wine-stains, or of certain seaweeds when they are first washed up. And there was so much motion in it; the whole country seemed, somehow, to be running."

As we drove further into Nebraska and I scanned Ann's old copy of *My Ántonia*, I came to see how the book didn't merely reflect the landscape; it revealed the state's deepest secrets, penetrating the veil of shy Nebraska's most intimate nature with almost embarrassing sensuality. It was as though Cather had stormed in from the fields to cast back some small farmer's flour-sack bedroom curtains and there the author found Nebraska sprawled out upon the satin pillows, stripped of her flattening, plain-print frock; and naked underneath, she was ripe, fervent, and bodaciously curvy.

Nebraska, state of the steamy sensualists.

On the outskirts of Red Cloud, Nebraska, Willa Cather's hometown, we pulled to the side of the road and strolled for an hour through the Willa Cather Memorial Prairie, 610 acres containing hundreds of varieties of grass, now preserved by the Nature Conservancy. The sun held high at about three o'clock; the temperature had hit 108 degrees. Ann told me it was the kind of day she used to call "close" as a kid, when the air stands as thick as water. The waist-high grasses whipped our bare arms and legs, and as we moved slowly through the fields we both felt as though we were swimming.

~~~~~

In Nebraska, people talk constantly about the weather. Nebraskans chew over the temperature, humidity, daily wind-chill factor, barometer readings, cloud formations, rainstorm divinations, flashflood warnings, and tornado preparations with an abiding, quiet fascination that borders on mania because the weather in Nebraska can no more be ignored than a time bomb ticking at the breakfast table. (If our moustaches iced over in February and funnel-shaped columns drawn to the earth from cumulonimbus clouds swirled at three hundred miles per hour to flip the roofs off our houses like shoebox lids, we'd talk about the weather in California too!) The mistake is to think that obsessive concern for rain, snow, wind, and sun is somehow indicative of an unimaginative or desperate people. The Nebraskan character, founded upon the unglamorous virtues of common sense, reticence, compression, and reserve, adds up to one of the great national models of grace under pressure. A more appropriate reaction to the state's climatic highs and lows—and more critically, to the enormous risks compounded by the weather for tens of thousands of people who still make their living in agriculture—would be a condition of gibbering hysteria.

Nebraskans are gamblers, always have been. It's not that they're drawn to the showy, swaggering kind of wagers that Texans prefer, risking it all on the bobbling future of oil leases or two-hundred-acre feedlots. Too many Nebraskans risk it all every season for any one farmer to crow about his own daring; it's all part of the business, tacitly undertaken and quietly esteemed. Farmers figure on weather troubles as naturally as firemen expect houses to burn. Naturally, they like to talk it over whenever they can.

The romance of pioneering one of the nation's richest strips of farm-land stands at the heart of Willa Cather's Nebraska novels. But the inherent drama of the immigrant farmers' lives was far from obvious to the young writer at the beginning of her career.

"Life began for me," Cather confessed, "when I ceased to admire and began to remember." Sarah Orne Jewett, the great Maine minia-turist and Cather's early mentor, urged the younger writer along with the oldest advice in the world: write about what you know. Write about Nebraska. Yet it wasn't until the middle of Cather's life—she was thirty-eight years old when her first novel was published—that she most fruitfully remembered the struggle of the immigrant farmers and the extraordinary beauty of the landscape upon which they suffered and triumphed.

Eventually Cather would write in numerous guises about her Nebras-kan hometown of Red Cloud and its inhabitants. In *My Ántonia*, she called Red Cloud Blackhawk; in *O Pioneers!*, the town is Hanover; in *A Lost Lady*, Sweet Water; it's Frankfort in *One of Ours*; Haverford in *Lucy Gayheart*; and though *The Song of the Lark* is set in Moon-stone, Colorado, the small town is, nevertheless, once again Red Cloud, the familiar setting still "anchored on a windy Nebraska tableland" and "trying not to be blown away."

The Cather family first moved to Red Cloud in 1884. Young Willa wanted to leave immediately, missing the forests surrounding her family's old Virginia farm. (More rueful than amused, she would later call Nebraska "distinctly *déclassé* as a literary background.") But over time, Willa found that the landscape of her new home whipped up in her an adolescent passion to which she could surrender with all the heat and singlemindedness of first love.

By the 1920s, Cather's vision of the fertile, rough land upon which the new country was founded had made her one of the nation's most respected writers. F. Scott Fitzgerald wrote to her, announcing himself to be "one of your greatest admirers—an admirer particularly of *My Ántonia*." When Sinclair Lewis won the Nobel Prize in 1931, he protested that the award should rather have gone to Cather, and he compared her favorably to other famous Nebraskans. "Willa Cather is greater than General Pershing," insisted Lewis, "she is incomparably greater than William Jennings Bryan. She is Nebraska's foremost citizen because through her stories she has made the outside world know Nebraska as no one else has done."

Red Cloud, Nebraska, population 1,300, stands upon the drifting plains, about thirty miles from Kansas, in the middle of nowhere. At the tail end of last century, eight passenger trains traveling between Kansas City and Denver passed daily through Red Cloud, which was then several times its present size. In its own peculiar way, the town seemed to rest at the center of things, the locus of the thriving zigzag still twisting and bending the country into shape.

Today nobody would accidently find himself in Red Cloud. The old railway station serves as a museum; the passenger line stopped decades ago. Yet each year, as many as six thousand visitors drabble into Red Cloud for the exclusive purpose, as the town librarian offhandedly told Ann and me, "to go Cathering."

On our first day in town, Ann and I visited the Cather family home on Third and Cedar streets. The house where Willa Cather lived as a teenager is the centerpiece of Red Cloud's 190 historical sites that now make up the official "Willa Cather Thematic District." Since Cather's acute memory threatened Red Cloud readers with an unusually high degree of verisimilitude, the debut of each book had once been the source of considerable local anxiety. The wastrels, villains, heroes, and fools that peopled her novels could be readily identified as they paced down the small town's streets. "I am the husband of *My Ántonia*," proclaimed the character's real-life model when asked to sign in for admittance to a hospital not far from Red Cloud. In 1965, the Nebraska State Legislature swept aside all lingering apprehensiveness and proclaimed the entire western half of the county as Catherland, an energetic expropriation of the wispiest reference to any building, barn, schoolroom, or alleyway in a Cather fiction—and seemingly every edifice in which the author might have written, worshipped, or trod upon the carpet.

Inside the Cather home, we listened to a series of elaborate tape-recorded messages activated by push-button controls that strained to sweep everything from the furniture to the floorboards into the context of the writer's fiction. The tape revealed to us that the front hall and coat rack were mentioned in a novel almost nobody reads today. The attic bedrooms, where Cather had pored over her studies as a young woman, and the downstairs detritus of the family sewing machine, rocking horse, and empty baby buggy appeared in several short stories. It was a handsome Edwardian home, the almost-cramped quarters of the not-quite-prosperous middle-class. During the summers, 175 visitors are said to ramble through the house each day. For some reason, we were able to wander alone amid the extravagant memorial, thinking that Cather had been wise to abandon the prairie at an early age. No person could have stood up to such relentless inspection in a place where she had spent her entire life, nor have been celebrated so exhaustively.

When we walked into the Willa Cather Historical Center on cobble-stoned North Webster Street, the wisdom of Cather's leaving home was emphatically reiterated, oddly enough, by the museum curator.

"People sometimes wonder why anyone would build a museum to honor one person," the curator admitted, shrugging his shoulders in a lugubrious fashion that hinted that perhaps he wondered too. For several minutes, the museum curator and Ann talked about Nebraskans' suspicion of the outstanding person. Nebraskans, they agreed, have never much cared for show-offs. In Willa Cather's case, even her boostering of the state could be interpreted as showing-off. With so much ordinary work each day binding together farm life and small town society, any dalliance with extraordinary labors, such as literature, had to seem remote, impractical, presumptuous.

After answering some questions about the Cather exhibits, the writer, her books, and Red Cloud, the museum curator confessed to us that he had been transferred by officialdom to Catherland, curtailing a far more satisfying twelve-year stint at the historical site in Lincoln that honored John Neihardt, the state's poet laureate back in the 1920s and, more famously, the author of *Black Elk Speaks*. Although two years had passed since the curator's new posting, he was obviously still uncomfortable with his public role in Catherland. In this sense, he was perhaps the ideal Nebraskan civil servant, reticent of the limelight. Only when the conversation veered back toward Black Elk and John Neihardt, with whom the curator had spent a more insulated and happy past, did he brilliantly wake up, his face flushed and full of life. Black Elk was a Nebraskan treasure whose value the curator could estimate. About Cather, he could only ponder and glumly say, "It seems like the land overshadowed her characters."

Of course, he'd skipped over the point, or rather the soul, of Cather. Bereft of the land, Cather's characters were unimaginable; she needed

Nebraska as Balzac depended upon Paris, as Dickens required London. But she did not resort to the land because she knew nothing else. Willa Cather was an immensely sophisticated woman; she lived for years in New York, chiefly amid Greenwich Village's own bohemians. She'd been photographed by Steichen; when she won the Pulitzer Prize for *One of Ours*, her novel about World War I, she appeared on the cover of *Time*. In Europe, too, Cather was a recognized figure. In England, she rubbed shoulders with H. G. Wells, Edmund Gosse, G. K. Chesterton, and John Galsworthy. She sat with Yeats and Lady Gregory in their box seats for the Abbey Players' premiere performance. Tomas Masaryk, the first president of Czechoslovakia, read all of her books. And when, at the Grand Hotel in Aix les Bains, Cather met Flaubert's aged niece, it was the midwestern American lady who bent over to kiss the old woman's hand.

Later that afternoon, Ann and I strolled to the edge of Red Cloud to watch the sun slip into a swaying, knee-high field of alfalfa, and I better understood why Cather had valued Nebraska so highly from the distance of Greenwich Village. It's not just that sunset over a glistering field of grain can be lovely. In this part of Nebraska, where there seems to be nothing *but* waves of grain rolling back into an unreachable horizon, the landscape feels everlasting, abundant, and, somehow, intensely moral.

At the edge of this alfalfa field, I thought I grasped for the first time why people twenty years ago in the Midwest—there, particularly— threw up their hands in disgust and confusion over the young people who collected most noticeably on either coast to decry America's corruption in Vietnam. Upon Nebraska's sublime, resplendent, and harmonious landscape (words that nobody would use, but everybody feels) such talk about American malevolence, our nation's original sins blistering into a field of evil, had to sound fundamentally screwball. The most obvious argument against the young radicals was the land itself: *just look at it!* No other country had repaid its people so generously for the cultivation of its raw potential. America was too abundant to be malignant, too much the beautiful woman above suspicion.

We like to pretend we're an innocent people. And even now, it seems as though small-town America largely perceives the country's present decline as pertaining exclusively to the jungle of cities. But out here in Nebraska, in the midst of the most generous and yielding landscape, the fierce sun shines through this illusion like blood on parchment.

~~~~~~

Back in California, it's always easy to get Ann talking about her fellow-Nebraskan Charlie Starkweather.

In 1957, Charlie Starkweather, seventeen years old, left his home in Lincoln, Nebraska, to ramble around the state for two months with his fifteen-year-old girl friend, gunning down nine people for no reason at all. When Starkweather was finally captured, Ann's father was serving as a district judge, and he'd actually caught a glimpse of the murderer in jail. For that reason at least, Starkweather is lodged in her memory.

One evening, shortly after Ann and I had first met, we were invited to a dinner party with three other couples whom neither of us really knew. At some point, Ann became heatedly, though mistakenly, convinced that the gabby architect sitting across from her was talking about Nebraska's most infamous criminal, rather than the fact that the skiing that winter in Colorado had been compromised by rude weather that he characterized as inhospitably chilly—and stark.

"He wasn't in Colorado," Ann told the architect, speaking above the dull hum of polite table talk. "Just Nebraska. They caught him in Wyoming."

"Pardon me?" asked the architect.

"Starkweather. Martin Sheen played him in the movie *Badlands*, did you ever see it? Sissy Spacek was the girlfriend. They killed nine people."

"Who's that?" asked our hostess.

"Martin Sheen," answered somebody else at the far rim of the table, hoping to squirm into the conversation. "He just killed somebody."

"That was Brando's son."

"He killed nine people. With Sissy Spacek's help."

"Martin Sheen, the actor?"

"No, Charlie Starkweather. He was a garbageman in Lincoln, Nebraska."

"Is this a movie? I haven't seen it."

"Where was Martin Sheen a garbageman?"

"This lady said Lincoln, Nebraska, of all places. I'm sorry, I didn't get your name."

"Ann," she said, "but it was Charlie Starkweather who shot all those people."

"Martin Sheen's sons were in a movie about two garbagemen, but I didn't see it either."

"No, Starkweather. Charlie Starkweather. He's from Nebraska."

"You don't ski, do you?"

"Martin Sheen killed Charlie Starkweather?"

"All I said was that it was rather stark weather out in Vail this winter."

"No, the other way around. Some guy named Starkweather killed Martin Sheen."

"Oh, my God! When?"

"Why?"

"It's just a movie."

"No, it's the weather."

"No," exclaimed Ann righteously, "this really happened. It happened in Nebraska, where I grew up. I can't believe you people don't know about Charlie Starkweather. I wasn't even born in California and I can quote you chapter and verse about people like Jim Jones and Charles Manson."

The table quieted down because she was really quite upset, and besides, nobody actually knew us. Nebraska, the ignominiously ignored. But folks can't keep quiet for long.

"Is Martin Sheen making a movie about Charles Manson?" asked the architect.

"This lady from Nebraska said it's called *Chapter and Verse*."

Over the salad, Ann whispered in my ear: "I'm really tired, can we go home now?"

When Bruce Springsteen released *Nebraska* (his somber acoustic album with the black-and-white cover photo, whose title song concludes with Charlie Starkweather's soul being hurled into the "great void" via the state penitentiary's electric chair), the singer explained that he'd fallen under the influence of Flannery O'Connor's short stories. But Springsteen could have read Willa Cather to the same effect.

Cather never amended her memories of Nebraska to fashion a sentimental Middle America. In her fiction, the edenic days of childhood on the farm are penetrated by the slippery entrance of vipers. Dispirited, incompetent farmers shoot themselves in the unforgiving winter. In the fall, crops can fail and families starve. (A mean, hungry Charlie Starkweather might have prowled around Red Cloud, Blackhawk, Hanover.) The story in *My Ántonia* about the pair of Russian bachelor farmers who throw the bride and bridegroom from their wedding party's sleigh to a pack of ravenous wolves is as barbarous and more believable than any horror tale conceived in the cities for today's jaded movie audiences.

That's the difficulty with remembering the places from which we've sprung: from the distance of years, we squint so hard as to make our upbringing all one thing or the other. It's all bounteous heartland or it's all stark, ominous plains. Cather looked in both directions; that's part of her greatness. She never indulged herself in the national amnesia that strikes our country with such terrible ferocity and frequency. Her fictional Nebraska is a booming, contradictory place—a portrait of the bustling human comedy underscored by the emptiness of the prairies. Cather once remarked that she had taken the small themes of rural life that hid in the grass and then woven them into the landscape's larger story, including its uncelebrated harm, mischief, and buffoonery. Like Dvořák's *New World Symphony*, inspired in part by several weeks the Czech composer had spent in Nebraska during the 1880s, Cather's memory wells up grandly enough to contain both her state's isolation and its solitude, the arbitrariness of sudden death as well as the land's insistent rebirth. Everything good and bad grew there.

~~~~~~

Throughout her life, Cather often came back home to Nebraska. Usually she returned to Red Cloud at Christmas and again for three or four weeks during the hot, sulky summers. During one visit she was urged to deliver a lecture to the women's club in nearby Hastings; she spoke then not of books and writers, but of the "Conservation of Native Timber," defending the much-abused cottonwood tree. Many Nebraskans consider their cottonwoods to be "dirty," but Cather assured the ladies of the club that across the Atlantic Ocean, Parisians held fetes in the trees' honor, celebrating the annual flight of their "summer snow."

In Cather's own fiction, the abounding cottonwoods glimmer, but never litter. "Trees were so rare in that country," she wrote about her childhood home, "and they had to make such a hard fight to grow, that we used to feel anxious about them, and visit them as if they were persons."

Yet despite the celebrated author's repetitious visits to Red Cloud, Cather feared that every time she went home, she might not escape alive. She fretted, like the slickest city dweller, about dying "in some cornfield." When Cather did die, at the age of seventy-three, her tombstone drew its epitaph from *My Ántonia*: ". . . that is happiness; to be dissolved into something complete and great." She was buried not in some cornfield, but rural New Hampshire.

Nebraska seems to be one of those places that you leave in order to love. Nebraska, the adored and abandoned.

From Red Cloud, it's less than a half-day's drive to Beaver City, where Ann's grandparents had lived for decades. They were both dead now, but Ann wanted to see the town once again. Beaver City consists of seven square blocks, and its population is about half the size of Red Cloud—another puddle of a town evaporating under the Nebraska sun. We arrived around dusk, following into town a trail of rolling hills lined with patches of sunflowers and hollyhocks. In the distance, cottonwoods sparkled along the horizon's rim, and cicadas hummed like rattlesnakes in the trees. When the lightning bugs swarmed, the darkening road was suddenly illuminated by what looked like an air force of floating light bulbs.

We found Ann's grandparents' house and walked right up to the front door.

On the porch, behind the screen door, the old woman who lived there greeted us warmly and urged us inside. She was a newcomer to Beaver City, having arrived less than twenty years earlier; she hadn't known Ann's grandparents. We wandered through the house's crooked hallways, inspecting each room. Finally Ann mounted the ladder to the attic, where she and her grandmother years before had unwrapped the wedding dress from its sun-cracked wrapper of plastic. To fit under the attic's drooping eaves, she had to fold herself in half at the waist.

"I'd think about selling the house," the old woman told us, "if I could ever find a buyer." In the living room darkened with heavy muslin curtains, we sat chatting and sipping tea. "But these days, people only seem to move out of Beaver City." And then more confidentially, "The house must be worth at least eleven thousand dollars."

After a half-hour or so, Ann graciously thanked the old woman for taking two strangers into her home. We stood at the front door shaking hands and exchanging addresses.

As we strolled past the front yard's summer garden, Ann said, "It's not what I remember."

"Isn't it the right house?"

"Yes, well, I suppose it is—as much as that's possible after all these years. But I remember something else, something different. I can't say what."

We wandered down to the town square and sprawled upon the lawn for an hour to watch the fireflies. I bought an apple and a bottle of beer from the market across the street for dinner. When I returned, Ann suddenly scrambled to her feet and pointed to a large sign hanging above a storefront at the edge of the square. The sign read: Beaver City Locker. She grabbed my hand and pulled me down the block.

The Beaver City Locker is the town's cold storage for slaughtered livestock. Ann explained that her grandfather had taken her to the meat locker as a child to pick up portions of some cow or pig chopped up and stored in the freezer throughout the year to be parcelled out for Sunday dinners. Almost every family in town had their own locker drawer in the freezer compartment and their own set of keys.

We stepped inside to watch two young men and a young woman hack and saw ribbed slabs of splayed carcasses. The entire enterprise consisted of one small carving station equipped with several stainless-steel butcher blocks and a huge refrigerator banking the deep-freeze.

"We don't get a lot of people asking to visit the meat," admitted the young man who seemed to be in charge. He swiped his cleaver into a loin of veal. "But sure," he told Ann, "go right in."

The heavy locker door swung open. Inside the refrigerated vault, we found a whole scalded pig and marbled strips of beef dangling upon their sharpened metal hooks. The locker felt unbearably chilly. It stank of blood, flesh, and refrigerated air. Ann turned to me, grinned innocently, and said, "It's funny what you can't forget." She drew a huge breath, stretching her arms up towards the butchered pig's snout as though she were a spreading cottonwood reaching for the sun on the most fragrant summer's day, and she refilled her lungs with memory.

ROUGHING THE TRUTH
WITH MARK TWAIN

I shall always confine myself to the truth,

except when it is attended with inconvenience.

—Mark Twain, a statement of editorial principles
  upon founding a newspaper in 1869

One weekend several years ago, I drove over the Nevada state line, into
Mark Twain territory, to meet an old friend.

My car waffled across the parched sage flats that run to the foot
of the Sierra Nevada; then it strained and lurched over the barren
peaks toward Virginia City. Twain had once remarked that these high,
scraped-dry slopes "looked something like a singed cat." Time had not
improved them.

For all of Twain's complaints, his own presence in the Territories, as
Nevada was called before statehood, only worsened the scenery. Not
only had Twain joined the legion of miners who poured into the Sierra

Nevada during the 1860s after the Comstock silver strike, leaving the hillsides gouged and potted, their empty incisions glaring raw and grisly for the next several millennia; he had also burned down the woods banking Lake Tahoe. On a weekend camping trip, Twain and a companion had let their campfire roar out of control. Minutes later, they were rowing out into the middle of the lake for safety, watching the conflagration consume the forest.

Burning down the woods didn't make Twain feel guilty. Rather, he thought it funny. Another example of the appalling distance between what the world *should* be and what it is: Twain's own definition of humor.

"On the north the eye falls on mountains," read an unsigned item in Twain's newspaper, the *Territorial Enterprise*, "looking east, the view is more varied and we see—mountains; turning toward the south we are again delighted with mountains, and paying our addresses to the west the monotony of the scenery is beautifully interrupted by mountains. . . . In short, which ever way we turn, the eyes meet a waste or a Sierra— range beyond range, till they fade away and are lost in the shadows of the distance."

Not far from this masterpiece of desolation, I had agreed to meet my old friend, Sandy Fitzgerald. We planned to rendezvous in the garish recreation of Virginia City, the boomtown that had given Twain his start in letters.

William Dean Howells once penned a description of Mark Twain, and in many ways it reminded me of Sandy. "He glimmered at you from the narrow slits of fine blue-greenish eyes, under branching brows," wrote Howells, "which with age grew more and more like a sort of plumage, and he was apt to smile into your face with a subtle but amiable perception, and yet with a sort of remote absence: you were all there for him, but he was not all there for you."

In truth, there was little about Mark Twain that did not echo through the life of Sandy Fitzgerald.

I first met Sandy in Tennessee, where we had both been hired to write "insider guides" to places we had never seen.

Our employer was a small start-up publishing company called Simple Pleasures, its main editorial office hunkered down at the foot of the Great Smoky Mountains about ten miles from downtown Knoxville; that is, it lay several light years away from every significant urban American social, political, economic, scientific, athletic, aesthetic, and commercial endeavor that enlivened the 1970s. There was nothing to distract us from our daily workplace tasks of fabricating reveries over better places to be.

The staff at Simple Pleasures was composed almost entirely of recently displaced big-city graduates from second-string journalism schools in New York, Chicago, New Orleans, Los Angeles, and San Francisco. As bachelors and masters of the trade, none of us had imagined that we would so rapidly descend into the lower depths of commercial journalism to churn out five-thousand-word commissioned puff pieces celebrating Hardcheese, Wisconsin, as "The Flea Market Capital of the World," or extolling the arteriosclerotic taco joints compacted like flecks of concrete cholesterol along the main drag of Gas Stop, New Mexico, as "the best bargain outlets for southwestern regional cuisine." At the start of our first jobs in journalism, we envisioned ourselves tapping out trenchant analyses of American culture and politics in the white heat of crusading I. F. Stone–*Front Page*–Woodward/Bernstein newspaperman style. But at Simple Pleasures, the most diluted efforts in this direction were immediately chicken-scratched with our editor's comments demanding a rewrite to "*Put more grin into this.*"

Our publishers had anticipated the conservative thrust of the forthcoming decade, in which Americans would long to crow about their country. What Simple Pleasures did was provide a free handout magazine that appeared to be specially tailored to each town, enabling citizens not merely to crow about the nation, but to celebrate their own justly unknown community in high-flying phrases that no honest person had ever used since its founding. At the editorial offices, we patched together the usual staples of consumer journalism (service articles on how to buy the most expensive stereo sound system, self-administered psychological tests to determine whether the reader should apply for an American Express card, and the like) and fit these offerings between a standard glossy cover stamped with the banner slogan:

SIMPLE PLEASURES
CELEBRATES LIVING IN
DEAD END, NORTH DAKOTA.

or wherever.

About two hundred cities and small towns bought into the gimmick. The bill was usually paid by an ambitious chamber of commerce, local college, or new car dealership. The inside copy for each community's edition was identical, except for the lead story, which was a guide aimed to persuade newcomers that their recent relocation from the scenic coast of Malibu to the suburbs of Powertool, Indiana, was not the most colossal error of their lives. These insider guides were always penned by local correspondents, usually college students, home on summer break, who had grown up in the community and therefore bore against it an enormous grudge. I was assigned to rewrite these pieces whenever our correspondents veered too close to the truth.

Sandy Fitzgerald was Simple Pleasures' head writer. He was thirty years old, tall and bony, with pale, sunken cheeks that gave the impression of a poetically consumptive hound. Nevertheless, I think everybody in the office thought him handsome, and also rather dangerous. His eyes were always lively and eager, painfully bright blue. His blond curls dropped to his collar, and his walrus moustache, more red than blond, bristled down to his lower lip. Sandy's clothing always included one piece of artifice—an umbrella on sunny days, a wide-brimmed hat, and even once a cape.

Although financial circumstances had reduced him for the moment to hack work, Sandy still thought of himself as something much finer than a journalist or whatever it was that the rest of us imagined ourselves to be. He was at heart a romantic dabbler in truth and beauty—he was a litterateur. Unlike Simple Pleasures' other staff, who had come of age during Watergate, Sandy had no desire to pore over secret documents, congregate at midnight with highly placed unnamed sources, right public wrongs, or even bring down presidents. All he wanted was to spend his life reading, pondering, and, most of all, talking about books and writers—and one writer in particular.

On the day we first met, Sandy informed me that when he was my age, he had ranked as "the nation's leading undergraduate Twain scholar."

I was curled up on our office building's cement steps, eating a cold bagel dog and reading *The Adventures of Huckleberry Finn*. Throughout my first week at work, during the lunch breaks, I had been sucking up chapters of this great book like snakebite antidote to the poisonous malarkey we were manufacturing at our desks during the rest of the day. No doubt my choice of authors is what prompted Sandy's confidence and, thereafter, his friendship.

Over beer and bourbon in the evening, Sandy gradually explained how he, like Mark Twain, had descended into journalism from loftier realms.

He had started out after college as a teacher, which then seemed the only possible way to dwell upon his necessary books and get paid for it. From the start, Sandy encouraged his senior English students to address him by his first name. The lesson was democracy. If they didn't want to come to class, fine, he wasn't overseeing an academic gulag, he didn't believe in *compelling* a love of literature. Go home, he really meant it; find something better to do; liberate yourself: *go away.* . . .

One morning in the midst of his first semester on the job, Sandy arrived to execute a lesson—*teach,* he assured me, was not the proper verb—that he believed would establish once and for all in the collective mind of his ass-dragging students why Mark Twain was truly the Lincoln of our Literature. But nobody showed up. They had liberated themselves. Few students came to class for the rest of the year. Sandy Fitzgerald was not a teacher, and he was satisfied to learn the news early in his career.

By the time I arrived at Simple Pleasures, Sandy had been sweating out copy for six months, mastering the compositional excess that made the job fun.

The problem was that quite often our local correspondents failed to glean Simple Pleasures' prime directive, which boiled down to *If you don't see anything nice, take another look.* On these occasions Sandy and I would delve deep into the corpus of their copy and disembowel its most negative insights. For example, if a correspondent reporting from Landfill, Louisiana, for some reason complained about the skies being slabbered with the rainbow effluence of his state's unrestrained petrochemical industry and then sourly noted that the caustic discharges of papermills and tire factories made his favorite lakes and streams bubble up and smell like nail polish remover, Sandy and I would amend the text to read something like, "Even a short visit to Landfill, Louisiana, will put you in touch with the dynamic quality of contemporary American industry!" When some gloomy young fool in Felony, New Jersey, noted that "only a madman would dare to ride the buses alone at night without packing a Magnum .357," we changed the copy to insist that "the town's wisest night owls always flock together—it's just more FUN that way!" Every evasion and lie concluded with an exclamation point! We came to think of this punctuation as a secret code.

Life at Simple Pleasures made us—the perpetrators—skeptical about the veracity of the printed word.

Mark Twain had also demonstrated a genius for dishonesty early in his career. His first writing job was with Virginia City's *Territorial Enterprise*, a boomtown paper of broad appeal, published to entertain as much as to inform its readers. When fact got in the way of fancy, Twain simply made up whatever was needed to sustain his own interest in the story. As he admitted years later, "if there were no fires to report, we started some."

From his first day on the job, Twain wrote mainly stretchers. The *Enterprise*'s editor tested Twain by directing him to wander around town until he could dig up something worth ruminating over in print. The young reporter noticed a solitary hay wagon rolling into Virginia City; he multiplied the wagon by sixteen, and brought them all into town by every which direction, raising local temperatures into "a sweat" over hay. When this elastic version of events prompted no complaint, Twain stretched a bit further. On another slow news day, he put some new arrivals to Virginia City through "an Indian fight that to this day has no parallel in history." Over the months, and then years, the reporter refined his talent for unearthing the nonexistent news and emphasizing its most intriguing possibilities.

Twain concocted "A Bloody Massacre" in which an imaginary miner was driven to a blubbering, murderous rampage, bashing in his children's skulls, felling his wife with an ax, scalping her at their cabin's doorstep, and then cutting his own throat and dashing to town on horseback to make his final, dying confession at the nearest saloon. Newspapers throughout the West picked up the story and ran it as evidence of the Territories' barbarism; thus, Twain's reputation extended from Virginia City to the California gold camps of Red Dog, Copperopolis, Grass Valley, and Sonora. On another occasion, Twain reported the discovery of a "petrified man" buried in the clammy recesses of the Comstock lode. Though the man was described in detail so that careful readers might glean that the impossible relic bore a wooden leg, a winking eye, and had positioned his hand in order to thumb his nose at eternity, less discerning editors carried the story without comment in newspapers as far away as San Francisco. Twain's hoax even crossed the Atlantic to appear in the *Lancet*, the distinguished British medical journal. By way of a retraction, the *Enterprise* ran one line: "I take it all back. Twain."

At Simple Pleasures, Sandy Fitzgerald carried on this tradition of his mentor, the old master, the old faker.

As the months passed, we ground out our mendacious versions of insider guides to abominable places, and the bonds of good taste that usually constrained our best exaggerations slowly unraveled. In one insider guide to Peapod, Illinois, or some other such place, Sandy slipped in a favorable comparison of the community's two-year agricultural college to the London School of Economics! It was just one line, but still—well, it seemed unlikely. Our editors said nothing. Sandy raised the stakes, claiming that the flannel shirts and denim overalls that had for years adorned the hardware store's seasonal sales rack in Eyesore, Alabama, were now attracting the most exclusive fashion designers from Paris and Rome who aimed to replicate the Eyesore "look" for le monde du haute couture! No comment from the editors. (Hadn't they noticed the exclamation point? Were they even reading the copy?) With every increase of exaggeration, Sandy grew more giddy. Any foolish notion he might concoct about these places was only batted back at him in print. There seemed to be no claim that exceeded the borders of editorial credulity, and Sandy's ambition to stir up trouble was consistently frustrated.

Finally, Sandy got fed up. He was supposed to be rewriting the guide to Cowtown, Wyoming, or some such place that our local correspondent had uncharitably dubbed "a vast suburban feedlot with convenience stores." Instead, Sandy spent the afternoon retyping the first eight pages of the 1974 *Student's* LET'S GO *Guide to Australia*, which made it sound as if the small Wyoming town had been settled by incorrigible criminals transported from the dungeons of Victorian England and that the surrounding prairies were now overrun with kangaroos. Near the end of the day, I overheard an irritated voice on the office intercom's scratchy loudspeaker demand that Sandy report immediately to the managing editor's office. But Sandy had already packed up his copy of Mark Twain's *Following the Equator*, which he was now studying during our lunch hour, and departed for good from Simple Pleasures without a word to anyone.

~~~~~~

Twain moved West to reinvent himself.

According to *Roughing It*, Twain's comic exaggeration of his western days, he had headed off to Nevada in 1861 to accompany his older brother, Orion, who was journeying across the plains to assume his post of secretary to the governor of the Far West Territories.

"He was going to travel!" Twain wrote of Orion. "I never had been away from home, and that word 'travel' had a seductive charm for me. Pretty soon he would be hundreds and hundreds of miles away on the great plains and deserts, and among the mountains of the Far West, and would see buffaloes and Indians, and prairie dogs, and antelopes, and have all kinds of adventures, and maybe get hanged or scalped, and have ever such a fine time, and write home and tell us all about it, and be a hero."

At this point, Mark Twain was still Sam Clemens; the pen name would materialize out West, along with the adventures. Like everybody else in the Territories, Twain was uprooting himself with the intention of striking it rich.

"I confess, without shame," he wrote, "that I expected to find masses of silver lying all about the ground. I expected to find it glittering in the sun on the mountain summits."

Instead, Twain soon found himself flat broke. He showed up for work at the *Enterprise* coatless, wearing a "slouch hat, blue woolen shirt, pantaloons stuffed into boot tops, whiskered half down to the waist, the universal navy revolver slung to my belt."

From the moment Sandy Fitzgerald walked out of the Simple Pleasures office, I knew that he too would someday turn up West. The West had sifted out the gold of Twain from the silt that was Clemens, and Sandy expected the same for himself. He talked about the West in the romantic way that is tendered only by people who have never been there.

But I didn't hear from Sandy for another two years. And then he wasn't West at all, but deeper into his own native South, working for a small public relations firm in Atlanta. Once again, somebody had hired him on faith—this time to secure notoriety for the self-aggrandizing upper middle class of the 1980s.

Sandy's specialty was sneaking items into the society pages by slightly stretching a point. If a prominent, middle-aged dentist had just returned with his family from vacation in France, Sandy might award him a private meeting with the Minister of Health. *Je vous ai compris,* the Minister of Health would allegedly tell his client, echoing the mollifying words of Charles DeGaulle to Algeria's *pieds noir:* I have understood you. The use of obscure historical references, foreign phrases, statistics, and nonexistent authorities proved particularly useful in placing his items with the daily press. It was the beginning of our nation's second Gilded Age (a term coined by Twain first time around in the 1880s), and fact-checking had lost its appeal.

But again, the old trouble arose. The public's eagerness to embrace the unbelievable drove my friend to unallowable excesses. Sandy spent his final week at the Atlanta PR firm composing a set of unlikely obituaries for all his clients, which he dispatched to the newspapers. (One printed obit referred to "spontaneous combustion.") Then Sandy handed in his resignation and headed to Washington, D.C., where he belonged.

One evening soon after, I met Sandy at the San Francisco airport, where he was being held over between connecting flights. I hadn't seen him for nearly five years, but I recognized him the moment he swayed into view near the baggage carousel, graceful and doomed, and just a little bit drunk. On his arm was a ravishing young woman, whom Sandy introduced to me as Pringle.

As we eased into the airport bar, Sandy explained that his new girl friend had actually been christened Shirley at birth, but as a teenager she had renamed herself after those potato chips that come stacked in a can: Pringles! Like Sandy, she believed that every American had the right to reinvent himself whenever necessary. She really was terrific looking, about twenty-four years old, sleek and bright—and I could tell from the exclamation points of false enthusiasm that punctuated her speech that she must be Sandy's latest protégé. They worked together as copywriters for Kornhauser, Kornhauser and Associates, one of the leading direct mail firms in the Capital.

"We've had an extraordinary day," Sandy informed me, as we stood at the bar, guzzling the latest Mexican beer. "Pringle and I have just been assigned to the new account for the American Hand-Gun-Control Campaign *and* the sustaining donors' program of the National Rifle Association. That's why we're out here doing the roadshow for our new clients."

"You're writing junk mail now?" I asked.

Sandy nodded modestly, and Pringle grew peppy and pert.

"We just got the numbers back on our most recent Ethiopian starvation package!" she exclaimed. "Nearly eighteen percent response! Everybody at Kornhauser, Kornhauser and Associates is buzzing!"

Sandy raised his glass in tribute to junk mail. I followed suit.

"Mr. Kornhauser," said Pringle, "Mr. Kornhauser *senior* told Sandy that the fundraising brochure, the pitch letter, the entire concept he put together for the starving children in Ethiopia was the work of"— she clutched at the air for their boss's precise sentiments—" 'a talented amateur who could one day turn into an old pro!' He said that Sandy's starving kids package almost made *him* want to contribute!"

"Who are you raising money for?" I asked.

"Oh, some new group," explained Sandy, clearly bored with the work even now. "Feed the Kids it's called. Before we got hold of their account, they were calling themselves Feed Their Faces or Stuff the Kids or something wrongheaded like that. Lots of gooey photographs on too-glossy paper zeroing in on all the worst aspects. You know, open sores, flies depositing their eggs on the kids' swollen tongues, that sort of thing."

"Oh, God!" agreed Pringle.

"And that's not the message you want to get across?" I asked.

"No way!" said Pringle. "Sure, it's a tragedy, but you can't alienate people!"

Sandy extracted from his briefcase a copy of the Feed the Kids brochure.

"It's a new color we're trying out," Sandy explained. "People respond very acutely to different colors. This one's called Buffalo Brown, which I guess is kind of ironic."

"Why ironic?"

"That's the whole point, isn't it?" Sandy seemed offended that I hadn't immediately grasped their strategy. "It's the message we're working to get across. There are no more buffalo in Ethiopia. The end of an era. So what can the tribespeople eat now?"

"I thought they were subsistence farmers who had been ruined by the war and the drought?"

"Well," said Sandy, "whatever."

The brochure was built upon three panels of four-color graphics, type-set copy, and lots of cool white space. It featured several action photos of women and children ladling out small portions of stew from a huge black cauldron that resembled the pots used to cook missionaries in the cartoons. The children held white paper picnic plates, plastic forks and spoons. They wore American baseball caps and smiled wanly like emaciated Little Leaguers. In the background, dusty-haired United Nations relief workers gazed on in horror.

"Who's the guy with the guitar?"

"Oh, Feed the Kids is put together by a bunch of rock 'n' roll impresarios who used to be cocaine addicts but now are busy promoting the hunger issue to get some recognition for their younger artists."

"You mean, it's all done to sell records?" I blurted out.

Sandy killed the remainder of his beer and stuffed the brochure back into his briefcase. He shrugged. He looked deflated. A Rolex was wrapped around his wrist; his Italian suit had cost as much as the car I was driving; his pink silk shirt and burnished, brown leather shoes were custom-tailored and imported direct from Savile Row and Singapore— but he did not look satisfied.

I had always loved Sandy's lies, but this was something new. I realized that he frequently did not know *why* he lied—what standing on the side of falsehood stood for. But in the past, his inventions had always been animated by a spirit of disinterested outrage. Now Sandy was dissembling with a motive; he stretched the truth to save the world and make a buck.

It compromised his integrity as a liar.

Twain, like Sandy, prospered during the Gilded Age.

By the 1880s, Twain had accumulated a shelf of ten books to his credit, a refurbished Connecticut mansion staffed with six servants, a wife from an aristocratic East Coast family, a brood of children, and expenses running about $100,000 a year. "Mr. Clemens," admitted his wife, "seems to glory in his sense of possession."

But Twain was also the son of a bankrupt, and he feared poverty all his life. By the age of sixty, he would be bankrupt himself—the victim of his lifelong misapprehension that his talents lay not in literature, but commerce.

Twain was an inveterate speculator. Over the years, he poured money into schemes to manufacture scissors for pruning grapevines; he bought a half-interest in a "bed clamp" patented to fasten sheets and covers around restless children; he worked up a child's game to teach history, his one effort that actually made money. Worst of all, he sank thirteen years and $200,000 into the development and manufacture of an intricate new typesetting machine that contained eighteen thousand separate parts, many of which frequently broke down. The typesetter was invented by James W. Paige, deemed by Twain "the Shakespeare of mechanical invention." By the time Twain abandoned the machine that had lured him to the brink of financial ruin, Paige was reassigned to the lesser category of "scoundrel."

Twain's humiliating public bankruptcy was overseen by his close friend, Henry H. Rogers, the chief architect of the Standard Oil trust— known to his numerous detractors as Hell Hound Rogers. "He's a pirate all right," admitted Twain, "but he owns up to it and enjoys being a pirate. That's the reason I like him." As a successful author in the East, Twain cultivated a much different set of companions than he had known out West in the newsrooms and bars. He became great friends with U. S. Grant, whose memoirs he published. Andrew Carnegie dispatched to Twain's basement barrels of whiskey as tokens of esteem and encouragement during the writer's most trying financial times. "The political and commercial morals of the United States are not merely food for laughter," Twain once declared, "they are an entire banquet." At this banquet, Twain was occasionally tempted to dine.

William Dean Howells shrugged off these contradictions, explaining that his friend was a "theoretical socialist and practical aristocrat." In fact, Twain's relationship to wealth had always been complicated.

Out West, he had witnessed the fantastic exaggerations that made unscrupulous men rich. In Nevada, the mine owners often toyed with the truth by keeping their crews working overtime, thus creating the impression of a big strike and driving up the price of shares. More brazen speculators salted their own mines with silver nuggets. In *Roughing It*, Twain mentions a claim enriched by melted-down U.S. government-minted coins; on one wall, the careful observer could still read the glittering inscription: TED STATES OF. Like many newspapermen of the era, Twain abetted these phony claims, albeit with an ironic flourish. He recalled in *Roughing It*:

New claims were taken up daily, and it was the friendly custom to run straight to the newspaper offices, give the reporter forty or fifty "feet," and get them to go and examine the mine and publish a notice of it. . . . If the rock was moderately promising, we followed the custom of the country, used strong adjectives and frothed at the mouth as if a very marvel in silver discoveries had transpired. If the mine was a "developed" one, and had no pay ore to show (and of course it hadn't), we praised the tunnel; said it was one of the most infatuating tunnels in the land; driveled and driveled about the tunnel till we ran entirely out of ecstasies—but never said a word about the rock. We would squander half a column of adulation on a shaft, or a new wire rope, or a dressed-pine windlass, or fascinating force pump, and close with a burst of admiration of the "gentlemanly and efficient superintendent" of the mine—but never utter a whisper about the rock.

In later years, literary fakery offered greater temptations. There was even a time when Twain thought he could prosper as a travel writer while he lingered at home, concocting his own insider guides to distant parts of the world that he had never visited.

In 1870, Twain dispatched an old comrade from his western days to the diamond fields of South Africa. Twain's confederate was a former gold miner and journalist named James Henry Riley. The plan was that Riley would spend three months in South Africa, collect whatever diamonds might be lying around (the pair seemed to have learned nothing from their overblown expectations in the Territories) and then return to America with sufficient exploits and recollections of the diamond rush for Twain to fashion a highly marketable volume of travel adventures. Twain envisioned Riley and himself eventually operating a kind of travel book factory, sending Riley off to "some quaint country," after which Twain would absorb his experiences and literature might commence. Riley journeyed to South Africa with admirable grit, riding four hundred miles to the diamond fields by ox cart along with ten thousand other prospectors. But three months later, he returned to the United States with not a single diamond to his name.

Riley may well have mined some great travel anecdotes during his sojourn, but we will never know. By the time he reached his sponsor's side, Twain was distracted with other projects. After seven arduous years, he was finally completing Huck Finn's own epic travels down the Mississippi. ("This summer," Twain confessed, "it is no more trouble for me to write than it is to lie.") While waiting for Twain, Riley fell sick and died, along with plans for the South Africa book and all future travel frauds.

In the spirit of this smooth-tongued summer, Twain stuffed his best book with tall tales, fantasies, hoaxes, and dire warnings about the author's tendency to exaggerate. "Persons attempting to find a motive in this narrative will be prosecuted," announced the novel's opening paragraph, "persons attempting to find a moral in it will be banished; persons attempting to find a plot in it will be shot." Yet *Huckleberry Finn* is Twain's book of candor and revelation.

Twain could not toss off the novel effortlessly, as he had with *Roughing It*, *The Innocents Abroad*, and his hymn to boyhood, *Tom Sawyer*. With *Huckleberry Finn*, Twain was attempting something new: he was diving to the bottom of the big river, which he understood to be truth. Always before, Twain's sparkling evasions and fabrications, his cleverness, had enabled him to skate over his deepest beliefs and convictions as though they were ice.

Now he found himself submerged in big muddy.

~~~~~~

Several years passed before I heard again from Sandy. During this time I worked for a San Francisco newspaper called the *Bay Area Badger*. The *Badger* was one of the "controlled circulation" weeklies, the throwaways, that had sprung up in scores of cities throughout the country. The principle underlying most of the weeklies was to slip around the breaking news (ceding that to the dailies) and the non-news (leaving that entirely to TV) to flirt with the Larger Truths, which might offer an instructive odd angle on ordinary life.

From the beginning, the *Badger* built its reputation by excavating the uncommon tale and then twisting it beyond recognition into a much larger parable for our times. The *Badger*'s dispatches on chickens that swim, or the decision of a local community college to give "life credit" for near-death experiences, or the man from the suburbs who raised gophers in his backyard only to harvest them in the spring for the most appalling kind of fur coat, all these journalistic coups seemed to wink back a sense of chumminess and shared conviction between the *Badger*'s writers and readers, boosting circulation, increasing ad rates, and spreading the message that whatever was wrong at this moment with the Republic, it was certainly not *our* fault.

The *Badger* thrived on controversy. And to keep the controversies pumping, we relied on letters. The letters column was the *Badger*'s life blood, its weekly transfusion. Only a limited number of people could be depended upon to read our massive front-page harangues regarding swimming chickens and the like. But almost anybody could penetrate a column of rambling, invective-filled letters. Our managing editor particularly valued the exchange of letters that ran on unabated for many issues—one correspondent hammering away at the finer points raised in the previous week's column. Letters covered huge holes in the paper that our publisher would otherwise have to pay some writer to fill.

At the *Territorial Enterprise*, Twain had also stimulated a large and wrathful correspondence. His most provocative story involved a fancy-dress ball sponsored by Virginia City's leading ladies. The proceeds of the event were destined for the Sanitary Fund, a precursor of the Red Cross, which supplied Civil War soldiers on both sides with clean bandages. Instead of covering the ball as a social item, Twain spewed out a bit of malicious fancy, suggesting that the evening's profits would actually be secreted to "a Miscegenation Society somewhere in the East." Sympathizers to the Southern cause reached for their pens, decrying Twain as "a liar, poltroon, and puppy." (Readers had previously characterized the reporter as "a miserable wretch, ass, fool, and idiot.") All this epistolary name-calling resulted in a proposed duel between Twain and his leading critic, but the deadly event never came off. Twain departed Virginia City forever, heading for San Francisco and shaking his head over the public's gullibility.

"To write a burlesque so wild that its pretended facts will not be accepted in perfect good faith by somebody," the author later complained, "is very nearly an impossible thing to do."

During my stint at the *Badger*, our most abundant correspondence was inspired by a controversial piece written by staff reporter Alma Ardilla. Alma's story concerned mosquitoes. She was against them. In seventy-five hundred words, Alma pointed out their defects—entomological, aesthetic, moral, and commonsensical—indicting nature itself for propagating the pests. It was a strong, unequivocal stand. Alma reminded readers that mosquitoes buzz, bite, and bother people. She sang the praises of household poisons. She expressed a personal preference for flies.

The letters poured in with their bizarre interpretations. As always, several readers judged the piece to smack of sexism, racism, classism, ageism, or—as was certainly true in this case—speciesism. A Berkeley Trotskyite denounced Alma as a liberal running-dog lackey of the capitalist media establishment (in six months the *Badger* would go bankrupt) for failing to provide any mention in her piece of the true aspirations of the working class to overthrow their bourgeois oppressors. A graduate student of political science specializing in North African affairs at U.C. Berkeley congratulated Alma on constructing a fluid metaphor that promoted U.S. understanding of the complexities governing the Polisario uprising in the Spanish Sahara—a place containing relatively few mosquitoes. The insect rights people took great offense at Alma's description of dismantling the pests leg by leg, punishing them for a long, sleepless night of buzzing and dive-bombing her ear. In response to Alma's praise of municipal mosquito abatement, one reader penned an antipesticide screed, quoting from Rachel Carson's *Silent Spring* at such length that our publisher had to consult the *Badger*'s attorney to determine if the newspaper might be liable for copyright infringement of the fair use provisions.

At the time, it all seemed pretty hysterical; but I now think that the weekly response in our letters column had something to do with preserving a fragment of personal integrity during the new Gilded Age's onslaught of lies. By the end of the eighties, many people had retreated from indignation over large matters of public concern into prickly personal certitude about issues that really didn't matter at all. Since speaking out changed nothing, we whined; we skirted the real issues, and lied to ourselves. It was this spirit of abdication and evasion that set the tone for life at the *Badger*.

On any day, I might sit in my cubicle, listening to the rickety false teeth chatter of clacking keyboards. To my right, Monk Abercrombie, the *Badger*'s resident movie critic, would be ruining the latest films by telling his readers in the opening paragraph how everything turned out in the end. Out there, somewhere, among the field of clattering cubicles, I knew that Alma Ardilla would be madly tapping out her latest investigative report—perhaps this time tackling the scourge of barking dogs on Sunday mornings or launching into another diatribe about parking meters. Food critic Les Clyde would be celebrating the newest restaurant serving pig's snout salad and pomegranate wine or some other trendy travesty. And Rose Studge, our rock music critic, would be embarking upon one of her long musicological essays about the contravening influence of pop music icons such as Andy Williams and Perry Como on the music of the Stranglers. Rose, to my way of thinking, was probably the *Badger*'s best critic. I actually read her stuff each week. I learned from it. Yet she would never be able to leave the *Badger* because of pervasive societal prejudices regarding her physical limitations. Rose Studge was deaf. Not that I think her deafness hurt her music reviews one bit. The true meaning of rock 'n' roll, she once explained to me, tended to seep up from the trembling, electrified auditorium floor. Rose gripped onto the music physically, with a kind of rapt, clawing attention that sound-distracted reviewers from the other newspapers could never begin to imagine.

One day, to these clicking rhythms of the alternative press, I was sorting through my mail when Alma Ardilla materialized at my cubicle's side and hovered above until I had to finally look up from my desk and face her.

"I got those bastards this time," she said, "those *readers*."

"What's that, Alma?" I was distracted by the postmark on one of my pieces of mail; "Virginia City, Nevada." No name or address appeared in the corner, but the handwriting looked familiar.

"I'm rebutting their wild claims about the sanctity of all living creatures. I mean, really, isn't there a limit?"

"You're still getting letters?"

"Hell, yes." Alma looked over both shoulders, crouched into a squat, and whispered in my ear. "Did you know those bastards spread malaria?"

"The *Badger*'s readers?"

"I am speaking of my nemesis, the mosquito."

"Everybody knows that, Alma."

"Yeah," she said, "well, I just found out. And I'm steamed."

"Now wait a minute." I dropped the letter onto the desk and I stared hard into Alma's face to see if she was kidding. "You mean to say you wrote seventy-five hundred words on mosquitoes—"

"—almost eight thousand. Not that I got paid one cent more for the effort."

"Alma, you wrote eight thousand words on mosquitoes and you didn't even know that they carry malaria? What did you say about them?"

"Didn't you read my story?"

"Of course not."

"I said plenty," asserted Alma. "Boy, I could tell you lots. Useless they

are. It shakes your faith," she complained, "in *everything*." Alma stared
down at my desk. "You get a letter too?"

I shooed Alma back to her own cubicle, opened the envelope, and
read Sandy's letter.

~~~~~

From the moment my car rose over the last mountain peak on Route 341,
I could spot the jagged rows of wooden A-frame homes and the church
spire towering two stories above the clapboard drugstore and dance
hall, and I felt transported back into the previous century—though not
in the manner that Virginia City's merchants and boosters had intended.

Virginia City is no longer Twain's town. Ninety percent of the city
burned down in 1875, and the structures now standing are the relics of
subsequent rebuilding. What does remain of the "flush times," as Twain
called his life in the boom town, is the spirit of scam and razzmatazz
that rises off the wooden plank sidewalks as barkers cull a quick buck
from the ambling tourists. Virginia City still thrives on its eccentric isolation; it is still glued together by avarice and baloney. Virginia City
may claim to be a living museum, but it is really a sliver of historical
curiosity grafted on to a sprawling main street of carnival sideshows.

Sandy had moved to Virginia City. His letter noted vague plans for
a book—an insider guide to the town that had formed Twain. But this
time, he had decided to actually see the place before writing about it.

I parked my car and wandered gleefully down C Street, past the Wild
West Museum, the Red Light Museum, the Gamblers' Museum, The
Way It Was Museum, all the way to the old *Territorial Enterprise* building, where Twain had sat, and scrawled, and lied. Twain had written
that "all mining towns . . . go up like a rocket and come down like
a stick." Virginia City had plummeted to earth better than a century

before. The rascals and miners had been replaced by ruddy tourists in walking shorts, most of them devouring ice cream cones. It is nearly impossible to put yourself into a Wild West frame of mind when you're surrounded by double-decker confections of rootbeer marble fudge and mint-licorice parfait; it's the basic nature of ice cream cones to undermine the spirit of frontier rascality. In an attempt to recapture the glorious past, I stepped into the pleasant gloom of the old *Territorial Enterprise* building, paid my dollar to visit its Mark Twain Museum, and climbed down the basement stairs to see where the young writer had begun his career.

The best advice I can offer anybody about this museum has to be, Don't Bother. It's anybody's basement with a steer's mounted head, old type casings, linotype printers, and scarcely anything at all specifically pertaining to Twain, except a framed oil portrait of dubious origin, a desk reputed to be Twain's own, and an ancient portable toilet with a stenciled sign strung over the lid: Mark Twain Sat Here. I don't know what I expected—probably not much more than what I found. Still, the place called up the essential spirit of deceit, hustle, blather, and con that once blew through every western boomtown—and I enjoyed it thoroughly.

Five or six other people wandered around looking somewhat bewildered. I heard a small boy ask his father who Mark Twain was.

"He's the man in the painting," the father explained patiently. "They named the museum after him." Satisfied, the boy ran up the stairs into the sunlight.

I was about to leave myself when another man called out from a darkened corner near the linotype machines. All I could see was the stranger's white suit, like Twain in the ghastly oil painting.

"Isn't all this grand?" he asked.

Although his back was turned, I could tell that the stranger was speaking to me, and when he turned and insisted, "*Really, isn't it all wonderfully shameless?*" I saw that the stranger was, of course, my old friend, Sandy Fitzgerald.

We shook hands and then embraced. "That's some costume," I told him, standing back to admire his vanilla clothes. The portrait of Twain glowered at us from across the room.

We climbed the basement stairs, stumbled out the door of the old *Territorial Enterprise*, and strolled down C Street to the Bucket of Blood, where we treated ourselves to a round of sarsaparilla. Sandy said he wasn't drinking any longer. In the light of day, I could see that his body was still a youthful collection of sticks and poles, his hollow-cheeked face still pale and canine. The only concession to age was the pewter bristles of his moustache. His hair now billowed around his ears like sagebrush, like Twain at sixty.

"You arrived just in time," Sandy told me. "The play's about to begin."

"What play?" I asked. "Can't we just sit here and lie to each other for a while? We haven't done that in years."

"No time," said Sandy, withdrawing a gold pocketwatch from his white coat. He explained that there was a troupe of itinerant Shakespeareans now rehearsing at the edge of town. They had fashioned themselves after the roving theater companies that used to roll through the frontier towns one hundred years ago. "Only now they work hard to make their plays more relevant to a modern audience," insisted Sandy. "This one is about drug abuse."

I'm sure I looked dubious.

"Don't worry, it will be great. I'm planning to devote a full chapter to these characters in my guide book. I forestalled the temptation to write the chapter on the plane from Vegas."

We walked outside the Bucket of Blood and headed down C Street. There was a makeshift stage set up at the end of the block.

A dozen actors rambled around a plywood stage raised three feet above the dusty street. Above the stage fluttered a canvas banner proclaiming, Shakespeare Was Clean and Sober. The performance began with a reckless facsimile of Elizabethan verse that could have rivaled the Royal Nonesuch. They were ghastly players, a fatuous re-creation of the West at its most bogus. Although the actors now seemed to be executing *Hamlet*, they had taken pains to blend into the mythology of Virginia City by dressing up in chaps, bandanas, sombreros, ladies' great plumed hats, and frilly dance-hall dresses.

"A new interpretation," explained Sandy, taking notes as the abomination proceeded.

The troupe fought its way through another excruciating scene. Ophelia tramped across the stage dressed up like a dance-hall prostitute, her hips gyrating ostentatiously under her red satin skirt in the style of Miss Kitty on "Gunsmoke." Hamlet moseyed in. He wore a ten-gallon hat and spurs. He chewed a long strand of dried grass, which the revised script enabled him to identify as "locoweed." When Ophelia expressed an interest in Hamlet's mental health, he bullwhipped her. Later Ophelia drowned herself in a keg of whiskey. The crowd was suddenly stirred by the histrionic performance: they lapped up their ice cream cones with fervor. By the final scene, in which Hamlet and Laertes face each other in a high-noon, fast-draw, six-shooter showdown, the crowd was completely on their side. The hideous denouement was accompanied by musicians on accordian and mandolin, adding a bayou whine to the Elizabethan carnage.

"Five stars," proclaimed Sandy, as we strode away from the travesty.

"You aren't going to *recommend* this spectacle in your guidebook, are you?"

"As we both know," explained Sandy, "journalism corrupts. Travel writing corrupts absolutely."

We headed up to the lonesome graveyard at the edge of town. The desiccated limbs of several scrub oaks spread their fingers across the sky like the hands of the dead. In his cool white suit, Sandy stood out like an improbably cheerful snowdrift against the gray tombstones of young men from Scotland, Germany, Minnesota, and Vermont who had died of fever, accidents, gunshot wounds.

The old faker, my old friend, seemed to fit right in.

As much as Mark Twain, Sandy had located his place in the world: he was forever compelled to mock the credulous nation whose disregard for truth in the pursuit of convenience could not be exaggerated. He was, of course, part of the problem himself. Lies, damn lies, and statistics, as Twain had said—these variations on the truth were Sandy's passion. Despite the distance of one hundred years—despite even the chasm that separates talent from genius—this is what finally drew together Sandy Fitzgerald and Mark Twain.

"How much time do you have to write your book?" I asked him.

"Oh, it's practically done. No worries. It will be out in the fall."

I didn't believe him. And as far as I know, the book was never published, never even completed. After I left Virginia City that weekend, the last I heard from Sandy was by way of an unsigned postcard, with the stamp in the corner marked "Peru." He claimed that he was starting a newspaper and if I wanted to learn Spanish, I could work alongside him as his assistant city editor, in charge of whatever I pleased. I kept the postcard, but never wrote back. Why should I? As Huck Finn said, I been there before.

INTO SOME WILD PLACES
WITH HEMINGWAY

He was always a little frightened of the woods at night.
He opened the flap of the tent and undressed and lay
very quietly between the blankets in the dark. . . . He was
not afraid of anything definite as yet. But he was getting
very afraid. Then suddenly he was afraid of dying.

—Ernest Hemingway, "Indian Camp"

When Ann proposed that we escape for a long weekend in the country,
I turned to a volume of Hemingway short stories to set my bearings.
The story I had in mind was "Big Two-Hearted River," an old favorite featuring Nick Adams, Hemingway's fictional World War I veteran,
recently returned from the Italian front.

Nothing much happens in "Big Two-Hearted River." Nick tramps
several miles into the forest somewhere in Michigan's Upper Peninsula.

He makes camp, fishes, cleans the fish, cooks dinner; before folding himself up in a blanket to sleep, he extinguishes a hapless mosquito that has lit upon the canvas flap of his tent. The mosquito hisses and flares into oblivion upon the nub of a match.

A summary of the story's plot falls desperately short of the excitement contained in the "big" Hemingway novels—say, Robert Jordan blowing up Spanish bridges in *For Whom the Bell Tolls*. Yet the small moments in "Big Two-Hearted River" have always meant a good deal to me. Ten years ago, when it seemed that everybody was logging sacramental time outdoors, I inserted a mental bookmark in my own memory, reminding me to consult "Big Two-Hearted River" whenever I began to lose track of the best reasons for spending a few days in the woods. I recognize that it sounds pretty foolish when a guy needs a book to remind him to go outside. But "Big Two-Hearted River" is one of American literature's most practical outdoor guides. It's also Hemingway at his zenith: not the swaggering bully of our worst recollections, slaughtering animals carelessly, boozing suicidally, squandering his great talent and years in self-parody. Rather, the story reveals what Alfred Kazin has called "the fierce love that Hemingway, beyond anyone else of this time and place, brought to Nature in America." It's this fierceness that has always drawn me to Hemingway, particularly when it's suitably rooted within the natural world, rather than paired to the domestic brutalities of the author's later life and lesser books. But despite the worst that anybody can say about Hemingway, the precision of every gesture in "Big Two-Hearted River" rings eternally true. Every time I read the story, I stumble upon something new. Or even better, I recall something I've forgotten, thanks to the distractions of everyday life in the city.

From his earliest moments in the woods, Hemingway's hero, Nick Adams, thwarts all distractions. Nick makes a study of his campsite, his careful discipline emphasizing a passion for order, the rigor for detail

that is the mark of a true outdoorsman. Nick's routine even compels us
to believe that a tin of coffee boiling over the morning campfire should
taste snugly delicious. Nobody drinks boiled coffee today. But the image
of the white-hot metal pot steaming over the flames reminds me pleasantly of a dozen sloppy excursions of my own into the woods and mountains with my buddies as a teenager and young man. I recall now that we
always let the coffee boil, burned the dinner over the campsite's stone-
rimmed ring of uncontrollable flames, and woke up in a haze of black
flies spread across a landscape of sand bogs. We weren't outdoorsmen.
And really, that's the point of once again leafing through the pages of
"Big Two-Hearted River": it's sweet to take a fluttery glance back at our
own first stumblings out into the wilderness. I can see three or four of
us now—rawboned, rangy, obscene teenagers—standing upon the curl
of some granite ledge, flushed with heat and discovery. We're perched
up there on that stony lip, out of the house at last and far from safety,
combing the woods for signs of life, maybe catching sight of something
small and puny like a rabbit or lizard—maybe ridiculously bumping
into a cow if we've strayed off the trail onto grazing land. And yet we're
thrilled to be there, callow and puny ourselves, sharing the view with
creatures we can mostly only imagine, trodding upon the vegetation that
we can't begin to identify.

It's the dirt-real feeling of this memory, coupled forever to one of my
favorite short stories, that I'll always cherish. And that's one reason I
agreed with Ann that we should leave the city as soon as possible and
get out into the woods.

Another good reason to leave the city was that the city we were visiting
was Detroit.

We'd just passed a week in the suburbs, handling some unexpected
family business. At the end of each day we circled back around the
city to locate our hotel, skirting Detroit's burned-out core of crum-

bling redbrick tenements and the flattened, flame-scorched lots that lay corner-to-side like chains of fractured dominos.

On our last night in town, Ann traced our escape route along the AAA road map spread across the hotel carpet, speculating which highway would lead us the farthest fastest. Ann advocated a trip to the Porcupine Mountains Wilderness, mainly on the strength of its name. She improvised a vision of friendly porcupine armies swarming out of the forest to surround our tent in the evening like trench fortifications. (In the spooky woods that neither of us knew, some spiky line of defense would have suited me too.) But a trip to the Upper Peninsula's western mountains could cost us another day, requiring passage that looped the far way around Wisconsin. Instead we shot past Saginaw, Bay City, Grayling, and Mackinaw City, straight across the gleaming arch of the Mackinac Bridge. I had another reason for urging us due north. If we headed to the Upper Peninsula's farthest coast, we'd eventually strike the territory described in "Big Two-Hearted River." Finally, we'd hit the Two-Hearted River itself.

Over the years, I'd told Ann more than she wanted to hear about "Big Two-Hearted River." I'd last read Hemingway on a solo camping trip to Northern California's Mount Lassen the summer before. And I had returned home from the forest full of praise for the same old story.

While it's true that many of Mount Lassen's cold-water lakes and wooded ridges resemble the territory described in "Big Two-Hearted River," I was otherwise treading upon shaky ground. Lassen is most noticeably a geothermal region, offering a ragged smorgasbord of topographical bewilderments not found anywhere in Hemingway: painted sand dunes, sage flats settled upon river canyons, alpine meadows melting into lava beds, gurgling fumaroles, bubbling mud pots, and devilish pools of boiling water. Patched together, it's a boggled landscape; no wonder the camper hordes haven't yet got a handle on what the place offers. Unlike Yosemite, which stands only 150 miles to the southeast, Lassen boasts no celebrated vacation valley clogged with ardent hikers, no famous luxury lodge, no afternoon gridlock. Neither is there any justifiable reason for me to have inserted Hemingway where he surely never stood, but that's how stubbornly the story could pull me back into its pages. It may sound silly, but it's true: whenever I found myself alone in the woods, I conjured up visions of Hemingway the Outdoorsman, patron saint to incompetent campers like me.

As we drove across the Straits of Mackinac and slid onto the Upper Peninsula, I droned on pedantically about the flora and fauna to be found up in Michigan—at least, as I understood it from my latest reading of "Big Two-Hearted River" the night before back in Detroit. Off the road, past Epoufette, we passed the charred remains of the previous year's forest fires, the poor-shave stubble of blackened tree stumps that brought to mind the devastation Nick Adams encountered when he hopped off the train near Seney to trudge past hillsides of burnt timber. In the story, Nick notices that even the grasshoppers were "all turned black from living in the burned-over land." The fire traces we encountered among the stands of sugar maple and yellow birch were not as severe, but they echoed the same hollow note of devastation—the persistent theme, as Nick Adams understands only too well, that wild country signifies "tragic adventure."

In truth, most wild places offer a great deal more tragic adventure than city visitors can digest. Back in Lassen, I recalled, the rocky flats spit vaporous sulphur and the mudholes bubbled up like campfire goulash. But Michigan's Upper Peninsula is a more subtle landscape. The forest throngs of trees, shrubs, ferns, and flowers press forward from the choppy, low-sloping hills and shaded river banks, not in a sweeping uniform assault upon the senses but rather as a succession of mysterious layers, peeled back at the corners or fanned like a fistful of playing cards.

First you notice the immense bouquets of hemlock and jack pine, and then the interspersed stands of black ash or balsam fir, and somewhere deeper into the woods you might finally stumble upon black spruce rising up amid the floating mats of murky-vert lake vegetation that the pioneering species had originally colonized. The dark forest is a thickset, lively place, and who can say what you'll find there?

In "Big Two-Hearted River," Nick finds a moment of peace amid a world of hazards. "His muscles ached and the day was hot, but Nick felt happy. He felt he had left everything behind, the need for thinking, the need to write, other needs. It was all back of him."

Ford Madox Ford rightly observed that Hemingway's "words strike you as if they were pebbles fetched fresh from a brook. They live and shine, each in its place. So one of his pages has the effect of a brook-bottom into which you look down through the floating water." In "Big Two-Hearted River," Nick also sees straight through our most popular illusions about nature. He has spent enough time in the Michigan woods to know that they're merely a temporary hedge against the outside world. Hemingway could never shake from his adult imagination the dark forest of his boyhood.

Even after he had finished the working draft of "Big Two-Hearted River," the unforgettable texture of the land forced him to confess to Gertrude Stein his desire "to write about the country so it would be there like Cézanne had done it in painting." Of course, the Upper Peninsula's devastated area, both in the story and from what Ann and I now saw spread before us, could never have been justly contained by the gauzy impressionists. Burned-over land demands Bosch or Brueghel, painters whom Hemingway also admired; all three artists were interested in fierce places. But in his longing to set it down on paper, I suspect that Hemingway was expressing the understandable urge of a man who both loves and dreads nature. He wanted to round up the wild things and draw borders around their persistent threat; he'd feel safer if he could wrap the wilderness in a printed page. I think many people feel this way. If not on canvas or in a story to be retold to the folks back home, then at least in our own indelible memories we desire to contain nature, though we know damn well that we can't. I suppose that's what *I'm* trying to do now: double-wrapping the wilderness in newsprint as I swab together recollections of my last stay in the woods with expectations for the next—with both dreams of the outdoors lashed into a single piece upon the fictional frame of "Big Two-Hearted River."

I know it feels tempting sometimes to bundle up the wilderness and carry it back home. But I also think it's an unsound practice and doomed to fail. The wilderness isn't just an idea. For the present, at least, it's still an actual place that demands our respect the minute we set foot there. That's what Dave Foreman, founder of Earth First! and an unusually rough-hewn environmentalist, straight out of Hemingway, is growling to whoever will listen these days. "It's not really wilderness," explains Foreman, "unless there's something bigger and meaner than you in there."

Hemingway was forever concerned about the lurkings of bigger, meaner things out in the world. In his fiction and throughout his life, this lasting anxiety led him to ask incessantly: Am I a brave man? It seems an odd question for a writer—by definition, a bookish person. Certainly the matter of physical courage doesn't come up much in evaluations of Faulkner, Steinbeck, Dos Passos, and the rest. But the unique relationship between Hemingway's work and the Hemingway myth makes it hard to ignore the question.

Was Hemingway a brave man? And if so, why does Nick Adams seem so frightened out in the woods?

Zelda Fitzgerald took an instant dislike to Hemingway, advising her husband Scott that the blustery young man from Michigan was "bogus" and "phony as a rubber check." Gertrude Stein, after being repeatedly wounded by the writer's legendary ingratitude, struck back in *The Autobiography of Alice B. Toklas* by calling him yellow "just like the flat-boat men on the Mississippi river described by Mark Twain"—a particularly nasty turn of the knife, given Hemingway's contention that American literature owed everything to *The Adventures of Huckleberry Finn.*

Of course, the rest of the world generally held a closer course to the Hemingway myth, the supermasculine re-creation of the writer as warrior, hunter, athlete, patriarch, and tribal chieftain. "He has the most profound bravery that it has ever been my privilege to see," wrote Dorothy Parker, in an uncharacteristically breathless and profoundly inaccurate piece of reporting for the *New Yorker* in 1929. Parker had fallen hard for Hemingway's war stories. Wounded by shrapnel in a trench shelling, Hemingway had amplified his injuries with nonexistent machine-gun fire. By the time he returned home to Oak Park, Michigan, he was telling friends, family, and reporters that he had been hit thirty-two times by .45-caliber bullets (he hadn't); that he was the first American wounded in Italy (he knew that he wasn't); and that he had fought in three crucial battles as an officer with the *Arditi,* Italy's crack shock troops (he had never even tried to join). All these fictitious reports survived in various scholarly and popular accounts of the author's life until Kenneth Lynn's debunking biography, published in the 1980s.

Yet Parker was right in essence, if not detail. Hemingway was a courageous person not because of the foolhardy risks he took all his life, but more because of the fact, as Norman Mailer once speculated, "that his inner landscape was a nightmare, and he spent his nights wrestling with the gods . . . that he carried a weight of anxiety with him which would have suffocated any man smaller than himself."

"As to Ernest as a boy," Fitzgerald confided in correspondence to a friend, "it is undeniable that the dark was peopled for him."

In rare circumstances, Hemingway could even admit it. In 1976, the great writer's son Gregory revealed that his father told him "about the times he'd been scared as a boy, how he used to dream about a furry monster who would grow taller and taller every night and then, just as it was about to eat him, would jump over the fence. He said fear was perfectly natural and nothing to be ashamed of. The trick to mastering it was controlling your imagination."

~~~~~~

We run to the woods to see what we can't imagine at home—or perhaps what we fear to observe too closely. But we still have to pack up and carry into the dark forest our old city selves.

By the time Ann and I cut a path to the Fox River through the bright flush of speckled alder thickets and the flowering bramble of blue flag, I had already been chattering away for several hours about Hemingway, Nick Adams, and all the devious ways that nature both comforted and terrorized the two of them. Ann had heard just about enough of that. She slid her pack straps off her shoulders, plopped the heavy bundle onto the ground, and rocked back against it like an overturned tortoise. She had her own book to stick her nose into.

Ann had come fully armed with a stack of terrain guides, each bountifully illustrated with trail photographs and precise, blazing-color identification plates, those *Baedekers* of birds and flowers. She studied her guidebooks and noted the profusion of wildflowers. She announced that seven hundred species of ferns, herbs, shrubs, grasses, and trees were gathered in Michigan's Upper Peninsula. They represented about seventy-five plant families. Even trying to separate one from another was hopeless. Wildlife fared somewhat better. The most common mammals were the low-slung, stealthy rodents whose relatives we'd just left back in Detroit. Alert and persistent, we might catch a glimpse of a rat, mouse, mole, vole, or shrew. A truly fortunate sighting would be a snowshoe hare or red fox, or, at night, perhaps a pine marten or lynx. There were black bears prowling and reports of moose and timber wolf.

The author of Ann's best guidebook expressed an expert's detachment from this profusion of wildlife. And he took even greater pains to mark his distance from the common two-legged mammals—specifically, the outsiders and know-nothings, city people like us. We should not get too excited, he cautioned, too *poetic,* about the outdoors and its accumulation of creatures who were, after all, only natural. His authoritative voice took relish in driving home the stiffest facts about the natural world's real character: the grisly truth was that all of the delightful creatures inhabiting our outdoors playground, this peaceable kingdom stretching from pine barren to sylvan glade, were at bottom hungry creatures, and they dined unmercifully each day upon one another's flesh, muscle, and bone.

We sentimentalize nature. But nature is no more a peaceable kingdom than Detroit: that is another message to be gleaned from "Big Two-Hearted River" with its burned-back woods and burned-black grasshoppers. As more explicit evidence, Ann read aloud an outdoors parable from her guidebook about the last bright morning of an invertebrate leafhopper residing along the Upper Peninsula's shore. It seemed that at sunrise this leafhopper fully achieved his own tragic adventure: he was eaten by a water scorpion who was then devoured by a lake trout who was immediately snapped up by a large garter snake who was subsequently gobbled down whole by a great blue heron.

Of course, all this murder and devouring is another reason we enjoy the outdoors. Close to the massacre, we can exercise our own rudest human nature. Naturally, we want to peep and gawk: it's *interesting* to stumble upon one creature munching up another. (I am always keen for campers' stories about how they were unable to turn away from the

spectacle of a wolf disemboweling a fallen deer with its furious paws.)
And that's because it's hard to justify this kind of curiosity back in the
city. After a few days spent in the barbarous woods, I think most of us
are glad to return home to the relative peace of urban life. The city is a
safe haven where our position at the top of the food chain remains taste-
fully obscured by the convenience of Safeway's meat market; where our
trout, unstuffed with scorpion, is wrapped in a sheaf of microwavable
plastic.

How smug and bloodless our own dinners must be—how distracted
the munching and crunching. Maybe that's why we find ourselves a bit
hungry after a time for all the bloody stuff.

Earlier in the week, before leaving Detroit, Ann and I had watched
a family friend perform in the ghoulish Stephen Sondheim musical
Sweeney Todd. In one of the most affecting scenes, Sweeney, the mad,
throat-slitting demon barber of Fleet Street, who stuffed *his* victims into
the worst meat pies in London, stepped to the front of the stage and
sang with piquant affection: "The history of the world, my sweet . . . Is
who gets eaten and who gets to eat." This line, noted our actor friend,
always got a great rise of recognition and revulsion from the audience.
Danger, everywhere, danger.

We venture into the woods because it's a great, dangerous place. That's
what Ann's guidebook, "Big Two-Hearted River," and our own instincts
insist we understand. And when we emerge safely, we're pleased and
confident. Maybe we're even a little astonished.

As Ann and I stumbled through a stand of dark-crowned hemlock,
sweating pleasantly in the cool shade amid the calls of warblers, wood-
peckers, and chickadees, Ann told me about an old boyfriend whom
years ago she had dragged through the northern California redwoods.
Fit and ruggedly athletic, the former Marine protested that he feared the
peaceable kingdom. She thought he must be joking. When they hiked

along the fern-patched trails, shaded over even at noon by the camou-
flage of the redwoods' cathedral bowers, he got shaky. Fallen branches
crackled underfoot: he wanted to turn back. Scampish ground squirrels
ricocheted across their path, bouncing furiously from tree trunk to burrow, rolling across the layered mulch carpet like hoppity grenades. Her
ex-Marine boyfriend blanched and refused to take another step; and
then he explained: Vietnam.

We slip into the woods for peace and quiet, and we find that. But we
also find the world at war with itself. Nature's wonderous complexity
turns out to be a code word for the constant state of siege. Ground squirrels and the sharp report of branches cracking underfoot remind us that
we're easy targets.

"Big Two-Hearted River" got that right too. Nick Adams, veteran of
the Italian front, finally cannot distract himself from his own bloody
experiences beyond the wilderness. In fact, the accumulated pressure of
World War I has long been held up as a critical key to unlocking the
deeper meaning of the Hemingway story. Kazin explains that "Big Two-
Hearted River" is really about "a soldier back from the First World
War, seeking on a fishing trip to empty his troubled mind." Nick's recollection of the war causes him to become "obsessively concerned with
every detail as he makes camp in a section of burned land." It leads him
to "the swamp" where "fishing was tragic adventure." Edmund Wilson
talked about Nick Adams's "touch of panic" in the Michigan woods; he
attributed the flaw in Nick's calm to "the wholesale shattering of human
beings in which he has taken part." Hemingway himself plainly stated
that the story was about "coming back from the war but there was no
mention of the war in it."

The story informs us that the woods—and the world—are wilder
places than we like to admit. We can find wilderness, places containing
"something bigger and meaner" than ourselves, wherever we go. There's

always something worth fearing out there, and it is by our own terrors that we come to know ourselves.

And yet, sometimes our terror is thrilling.

I'm thinking right now about some fellows I knew years ago from Deadwood, South Dakota, who scrambled through urban landscapes as though our cities were the wildest places on earth. I first met the Deadwood boys at a dull professional meeting in Salt Lake City. Warding off Sunday morning blue laws, they had imported several cases of beer for a wide-open hotel-room bash. Later they showed up in Oakland: hicks on the loose, they bragged. Most exhilarating to these rustics, veterans of the South Dakota high plains and prairies who professed admiration for the worst and wildest that the peaceable kingdom could throw at them, was the prospect of being killed in the city. They might be mangled on the busy freeway, fall off a skyscraper, run into the point of a mugger's knife because of their incautious hick detours. The jungle of cities offered them risks that home could not provide. During the winter, buried in snow back in Deadwood, they would lull themselves into dangerous dreams about the kind of wildness they missed on a daily basis. No longer on the loose, the hicks studied Bellow, Roth, Nelson Algren, and James T. Farrell for insight into the urban badlands.

Of course, books should open up all kinds of experience. They should pry us loose, nudge us into the country, cast us off into the city. But books cannot contain the whole story. When we try to preserve what we feel most deeply, most *suddenly,* between the pages of a book—a slick technique for smoothing out the fearful creases—we also run the risk of pressing flat the experience once the book is finally slapped shut.

Experience should leap out at us.

~~~~~~

A yellow-mottled cat leapt out at us on the two-lane blacktop skirting the Two-Hearted River. It had scrambled out from the brush and slipped under my car's left front wheel. I could feel the car roll up, then over, the cat's body. We pulled to the side.

Years ago, I hit a slick black Labrador retriever near my home. At the time, I drove a 1963 Chevy Impala. The dog glanced off its bumper, sailing wonderfully across the street. His haunches curled up towards his gaping jaws, his white eyes throbbed, and his pink tongue flapped with enthusiasm; he looked like a great heap of animated coal merrily cannonaded. When the Labrador retriever hit the dirt with a dusty scrape, he yelped once, galloped into his front yard, and frothed like a braggart while whipping his tail around the legs of his nonchalant master. The dog was okay, his owner assured me, no problem, no sweat, happens all the time.

Now, like everybody else, I drive a little Japanese four-banger: lucky for the cat up in Michigan.

She picked herself up from the road and shot back into the woods. It seemed impossible that she wasn't dead. Finally, Ann located her among the seven hundred species of ferns, shrubs, and grasses. She bled from the hind legs. I think she recognized us as her assailants: her eyes cried alarm, and she flitted back across the field, slipping into a drainage pipe. Maybe now she could nurse her hindquarters in the darkness, or die privately, miserably, from unseen wounds.

Our duty was clear. We had hit her, though of course, it had been an accident. But we were the cause of her pain, and now we had to make the pain stop. We had to rescue her. Or if the injury proved too grave, we had to kill her; in any case, we needed to stop her pain. But I think we both knew that, as city people, we might not measure up to the task; we weren't used to killing, even in kindness. And *how* would we do it? Ann might stomp upon the infestation of garden snails that each morning trailed across her flowerboxes back home, but how would we dispatch a creature that might have otherwise fit warm and purring in our arms? Finally, the cat proved impossible to aid. She had scudded into the pipe, knowing that two big creatures like us would never even try to fit inside. She would suffer in peace, her pain unmolested.

But something else sat in the road, fluffy and barely squeaking. A kitten. It's neck was wet, where the mother had latched on to carry it—before she slipped under my car wheels, before the kitten sailed to perfect safety like the fortunate black Labrador of years past. I scooped up the kitten and carried it down the road. There was a fishing lodge situated about a quarter mile into the woods.

The woman who managed the lodge speculated that I had hit a feral cat. We discussed taking the kitten back to the pipe, where the mother might return for it. But then, the mother also might die.

"Don't you want a nice little cat?" the lodge manager demanded feebly. We didn't even have to make excuses about living two thousand miles away. The woman was obviously a big softie. She cradled the kitten in her flat, open palms. It was hers already.

I have to admit that my guidebook, "Big Two-Hearted River," failed to prepare me for the tragic adventure of the cat and her kitten. Nick Adams never displays any fondness for the wild animals whose company he shares in the woods. The fish he pulls from the water can't be garnished with sentimentality; they're slated for dinner over the campfire griddle. Yet Nick Adams's creator, the hardboiled Hemingway, was a notorious big softie in some special cases. Although he butchered countless wonderful wild beasts throughout his life, more often for amusement than any good reason, he was ridiculously touched by—what else?—household cats. Throughout his later years, in Cuba at the Finca Vigia, Hemingway lived with fifty-two cats. Years earlier, during one of his black moods in Paris, the young writer confessed to a friend that he had "just one consolation" in life—and that consolation was "my kitty."

Even in the wilderness, even among the wildest creatures, sometimes we strike upon an errant kindness, unreasonable and unexpected, but right and necessary too. I am sorry I ran over the cat. I am glad the woman took the kitten.

Sometimes we go out into the wild places and find ourselves not only enlivened, but also softer and more vulnerable, even more sentimental than at home in the cities that have hardened us. Unprotected by routine, we see that anything can happen. We witness little lives snuffed out with hideous regularity: the mosquito blazing upon the flame of Nick Adams's matchstick, that poor cat, us too, eventually. It's hard not to think about our own inevitable end out there among the wild things.

In the evening, after the cat, Ann and I hiked back to the Two-Hearted River and briskly circled the perimeter before bedding down to sleep the night by the shore. Trout flipped in and out of the water, sewing together the sky and the river's broken surface with their comic, blunt needle-faces.

At dusk a family of deer boldly crept into the meadow. It was meteorite season, and the sky should have been laced with falling stars, but we forgot to look up. Instead we lost ourselves in belting out Broadway show tunes to the doe and its four fawns, an absurd salute to Michigan's Upper Peninsula, the big Two-Hearted River, and I suppose to Hemingway too. We sang corny songs from *My Fair Lady* and *Guys and Dolls*. Ann knew all the words to "Embraceable You." We both made a run at some cannibalism numbers from *Sweeney Todd*. We sang out with threats and admiration to the deer who paid almost no attention to us at all. Occasionally the doe would look up, wagging her head with anthropomorphic disdain. Then she cast an eye over her family and returned to her feed in the high grass.

ZORA NEALE HURSTON IN THE LAND OF 1,000 DANCES

God only knows what the world has suffered
from the white damsels who try to sing Blues.

—Zora Neale Hurston, "Characteristics of
Negro Expression"

Jelly Roll Morton once boasted that New Orleans contained "everything in the line of hilarity." As soon as I arrived in the city, I left my hotel in the financial district, crossed Canal Street, and wandered all afternoon through the French Quarter, listening to the streets that proved Jelly Roll right.

Squeezed into a perfect rectangle by the Mississippi River and three 270-year-old streets with their flowering of flagstoned alleyways and high-walled courtyards, the tightly compacted Vieux Carré, or Old

Square, stands at the heart of New Orleans in the way that the Medina defines Casablanca or the casino strip, Las Vegas. Music pervades the French Quarter, and the sounds of one block sprawl into the next. On the corner of Decatur Street, I watched a man withdraw a tenor saxophone from the green plastic trash sack slung over his shoulder and lilt into "Angel Eyes." His tone persisted in the air like the scent of smoked chicory until I ran into a klezmer band down near the market. In front of the stacks of blood oranges and plantains, the clarinet player wriggled through his changes with the same snaky invention as Johnny Dodds, the New Orleans master who set the instrument's standard in Louis Armstrong's bands, the Hot Five and Hot Seven. One hundred feet away, a luminous coal-faced teenager tugged upon the lacy pleats of her thrift-store evening gown, shook its sequins like stars, and flared an Edith Piaf torch song. At the Cafe du Monde, I paid close attention to the fattest man I had ever seen, squeezed behind a portable electric piano; he looked like a block of white marble topped with a beret, and he beat out the chords with his hammer fists to a Latin tune I couldn't recognize, croaking lyrics with as much Spanish as English, enveloping the entire song in a moist and lazy Cajun slur.

New Orleans is the city of all possible combinations. For nearly three hundred years, it has bound together the sounds of France, Spain, Latin America, the West Indies, and Africa. It's still the country's most *musical* place, the joyous noise of its divers parts rattling the sidewalks. And yet it all blends: the multiple overtone that rises off the streets seems less mishmash, frantic, incongruous, or adversarial than ingeniously complementary. American music, in spite of itself.

As the sun fell, I strolled back to my hotel. My eyes followed the waves of Spanish wrought iron rippling across the district's second-story balconies. At the front of one grand home on Royal Street, I stopped to admire a huge cast-iron gate of blossoming cornstalks, each post resting upon a pumpkin with the vines intertwined amid morning glories; at the gate's center, my hands lighted upon the iron butterfly frozen in flight. Shadows descended upon the sidewalks and the autumn air cooled. In the distance, I heard saxophones; or they might have been bagpipes. My first night in New Orleans, city of echoes.

By the time I reached the financial district and found my hotel, I thought I might read for a half-hour before falling asleep. After a day spent roaming the streets almost overfilled with songs, reading sounded like a pleasant idea, but reading wasn't possible because the songs hadn't stopped. Next door in the hotel, my neighbors were playing their music with a bass, booming, thunderous *hilarity*. And it wasn't recorded music, either; the walls shook with its liveliness.

Somebody on spastic bass slapped the instrument with fat, sloppy blows. An electric piano throbbed like a headache and a piercing guitar screamed occasionally like a high-intensity industrial drill. Above all this electronic ululation, I could make out the strenuous bleat of indecipherable lyrics, words piling up like a multicar collision into the monotonous rhythm of rap.

In my bathrobe and bare feet, I inserted myself into the hallway and hammered on their door.

The white boy who answered looked about nineteen, decked out in studs and leather, his blond curls dyed evergreen with splotches of red and blue that dragged to his shoulders like the drooping branches of a Christmas tree.

"Do you think you fellows could turn down the music just a little bit?" I asked.

My bare feet stuck out like swim fins beneath the bathrobe. The Christmas tree youth eyed them dubiously.

"I'm trying to read," I explained, holding up my book.

He silently mouthed the words on the cover.

Their
Eyes
Were
Watching
God
by
Zora
Neale
Hurston
"Never heard of it."
The walls undulated to a terrific squall. A bass drum pounded. The
Christmas tree shrugged. Through a crack in the door, I could see
their amplifiers spread across the room; microphones dangling from the
hands of a young black man who wore his hair in long, natty dread-
locks; white boys with guitars sporting spiky Mohawks and Parris Island
marine haircuts tinted blue. Keyboard synthesizers flattened their un-
made beds. I spotted them immediately for my worst nightmare: white
suburban punks and black gangster rappers joining together in an inter-
racial congress of all things unmusical. They were band kids probably
hitting the southern club circuit for the first time.
    "Who is it?" demanded the kid with the microphone.
    "I dunno. Some old bald guy from the bookmobile."
    I objected, but the door slammed shut. The kids cranked up their
music several more decibels. I ground my fingers into fists. Blood shot
up into my face like a thermometer. My desperate little plea: *I just want
to read my book.*
    But I knew that they would not turn down the music.
    I knew this to be true because, when I was young, I had played in
a band myself, and we had assumed the same unequivocal, ululating
stance towards middle-aged, bald-headed guys in bathrobes who wanted

us to turn down the music so they could read their books. The kids next door might turn down the music someday. But I wasn't going to be able to read another word until somebody convinced the kids in the band that *Their Eyes Were Watching God* by Zora Neale Hurston was full of music too.

Twenty years ago, hardly anybody had heard of Zora Neale Hurston. In the 1930s she had been an important figure in the Harlem Renaissance, publishing exquisite accounts of black rural life in stories, novels, and not-quite-scholarly interpretations of folktales—"them big old lies we tell when we're jus' sittin' around here on the porch doin' nothin'." Yet over time, her reputation had been dragged down by the currents of literary politics and fashion.

Hurston was a figure of the Great Migration, the decade following World War I when almost one million black people wrenched themselves from their southern roots and headed for the promise of prosperity in the big northern cities. They carried with them a rich tradition of tales, myths, and music—a unified way of life, a cultural *whole*, as Hurston had the insight to grasp and the genius to re-create on the printed page. This recognition owed much to the vitality of her childhood home. Hurston had grown up in the small, all-black town of Eatonville, Florida, and she "had the map of Dixie on her tongue." Eatonville lay only a few miles from Orlando, but it did not feel like an exhausted ghetto orbiting the larger, richer, more powerful white city. Hurston's childhood Eatonville was a proud, independent, self-governing, fully functional community: the model for her vision of black life in America. When she moved to Harlem, striking up friendships and rivalries with Langston Hughes and other artists of the era, Hurston took Eatonville with her; the rural South of her childhood stood out from everything she wrote.

After her death in 1960, Hurston's reputation as an artist was gradually erased. Her books ran out of print; for all but the most scrupulous used-bookstore browsers, the great body of her work remained unavailable. Hurston had always been most interested in places like Eatonville, where the people sat around after work "on the porches and passed around the pictures of their thoughts for others to look at," their "crayon enlargements of life." But by the 1960s, this kind of storytelling had become distinctly unfashionable. Among black intellectuals, Hurston was dismissed as a political reactionary or disdained as an opportunist who had forged her career out of professional folksiness.

At the heart of this rejection was the fact that, for many readers, Hurston's books skimmed over one obvious aspect of black life in the rural South: oppression. Hurston had rejected the dictum of W. E. B. Du Bois, who stipulated in *The Souls of Black Folk* that "all Art is propaganda and ever must be, despite the wailing of the purists." Not only did Hurston's writing fail to take aim at the power structure, but the black folks in her books did not even regard the whims of white folks as a significant force in their lives; they barely seemed to notice them. Hurston's best work existed outside of time. The people in several of her novels and folklore collections could have been living during the Great Depression or Reconstruction. Richard Wright, who raised the American social-protest novel to new levels of outrage and artistry, deeply resented Hurston's historical evasions. "Her characters eat and laugh and cry and work and kill," he wrote, "they swing like a pendulum eternally in that safe and narrow orbit in which America likes to see the Negro live: between laughter and tears."

It seems useless to argue the point; it's true. But it's also true that Hurston's books contain what most of her contemporaries could not or would not chronicle: the cohesion, integrity, and stubborn exuberance of rural black culture. "Hurston implicitly told whites," observed her biographer, Robert Hemenway, that contrary "to your arrogant as-

sumptions, you have not really affected us that much; we continue to
practice our own culture, which as a matter of fact is more alive, more
esthetically pleasing than your own; and it is not solely a product of
defensive *re*actions to your actions."

In 1973, Alice Walker traveled to Fort Pierce, Florida, to mark
Hurston's grave in an overgrown, segregated cemetery. Hurston had
spent her last days in the county's welfare home, and she died a pau-
per. Walker set up a gravestone that she had specially commissioned,
reading: ZORA NEALE HURSTON '*A Genius of the South*' *1901–1960
Novelist, Folklorist, Anthropologist*. It was a righteous act of gratitude
and recognition that neither the literary establishment, academia, the
publishing world, the NAACP, nor the NEA would ever get around
to doing. "In my mind," wrote Walker, "Zora Neale Hurston, Billie
Holiday, and Bessie Smith form a sort of unholy trinity. Zora belongs
in the tradition of black women singers. . . . There were the extreme
highs and lows of her life, her undaunted pursuit of adventure, her passionate emotional and sexual experience, and her love of freedom. Like
Billie and Bessie, she followed her own road, believed in her own gods,
pursued her own dreams, and refused to separate herself from 'common'
people."

Today Hurston's reputation has been renewed. Her books are back in
print. Plays by and about the author have appeared on television, Broadway, the London stage. Nearly lost two decades ago, she has now been
admitted to the pantheon of great American writers, standing solidly
alongside her most ardent detractors. Her rehabilitation is long over-
due. And rather than sounding dated, the booming, signifying, hilarious
music of her language has never sounded richer or more full of joy and
suffering or more urgently welcomed by readers born years and worlds
away from the heart of the beat of her life.

~~~~~~

When I was a kid, all the white boys in my town longed to sing the blues. So when my friends and I pulled a band together in our freshman year of high school, there was never any doubt that the music we would be playing was soul.

I lived in a small working-class suburb lined up along the Oakland border. Tract homes, built after World War II, filled with Italians, Portuguese, Irish, Mexicans, and Jews. Oceans of cement and grass-seed floating on G.I. loans. Three-bedroom, solid, stucco houses with a postage stamp patch of golf-course-green lawn and a slender sycamore bowing across the sidewalk.

Not one black family lived there. Nobody told stories on their front porches after work. Any way you looked at it, soul did not appear suited to the place.

My instrument was the tenor saxophone. I bought a pawnshop Selmer and fit the horn with a sleek metal mouthpiece, like the kind King Curtis used to blow off the high harmonics in "Memphis Soul Stew Serenade." Playing the saxophone encouraged me to listen harder for sounds I might have otherwise missed. Tapps, my best friend, was our band's trumpet player, and he heard things that *nobody* else seemed to hear. Early on, he clued me into a great secret: Musicians are the only heroes left.

As a teenager, Tapps covered the walls of his bedroom with pictures of musicians. Not just the usual stuff. Not the Beatles, Stones, Zombies, Animals, Herman's Hermits, Manfred Mann, Chad and Jeremy, Peter and Gordon, Paul Revere and the Raiders, Freddie and the Dreamers, Wayne Fontana and the Mindbenders, and the rest; not the stuff our sisters hung up on their bedroom walls. Tapps clipped a silhouette of Miles Davis from the Columbia album *Kind of Blue* and pasted it on a regal piece of purple construction paper mounted over his bed—

right below his childhood night-light that showed Mickey Mouse in magician's robes and a conical hat from "The Sorcerer's Apprentice."

Tapps was also the first person in our town to utter these words: *Thelonious Monk*. He whispered them to me on my thirteenth birthday at Washington Manor Park when he produced a soiled paper bag from the clump of scrub oak where the older kids nipped at their emerald bottles of Thunderbird wine. From the paper bag, Tapps pulled a copy of Monk's album *Brilliant Corners*, swiped from the old White Front discount store on Hegenberger Road. At the time, I was mainly hip to Dave Brubeck. Tapps wanted to point out that there was definitely something else going on, and it involved people who could not safely set foot in our town. He was standing up for Art, and he was often misunderstood. I'm sure Tapps could have sympathized with Zora Heale Hurston, if he or anybody else in our town had ever heard of her.

" 'Music is okay for a hobby,' that's what your old man is going to tell you," warned Tapps, just days before my dad did exactly that. " 'But you can't ever make a living from it.' *Pay no attention to him.*"

One thing every guy heard from his old man was what you could and could not do to make a living. Even fathers who never uttered ten words to their sons, fathers who came home sleepy-drunk from work every night, not fit to lecture the dog, even mean-drunk and dangerous fathers or father who just didn't give a damn about anything at all—fathers who choked to death on big chunks of barbecued steak at their girlfriends' secret apartments across the Oakland border, like Tapps's old man did when Tapps was just eleven—even the worst, most careless and irresponsible fathers got around to mentioning to their sons what you could and could not count on to make a living for you and your family.

Of course, there was only one kind of work that interested us as kids: the labor of packing up our amplifiers and instruments and heading off in our primer-gray '60 Chevys and fourth-hand Ford vans for the road. Every young musician's dream: the winter redneck club circuit that stretched from Sacramento up through Boise, Missoula, and Fargo, North Dakota. Night clubs and taverns where the patrons put the flourish on Saturday night by firing a round from their Smith & Wessons into the jukebox because the 45 of B. B. King and Bobby Blue Bland singing "Stormy Monday" skips.

Six of us formed the band. Tapps and I made up the horn section. Richie D'Vinio played lead guitar and also served as the band's leader. Nick Dunne played drums, and Reginald "Space" LeBlanc handled the bass guitar. But our greatest asset was our singer, Teddy Chavez. Teddy had a sweet, lacquered voice that poured out of his mouth like honey and seeped into the perforated hearts of all the teenaged girls. On stage, Teddy could pout, cry, plead, rage, and otherwise express the full range of his emotions in mannered and histrionic detail.

I mention all this to explain that we might not have known who Zora Neale Hurston was, nor cared to read her books if we had, but there was still nothing finer to us back then than righteous black music. We lived for the Temptations and the Four Tops; in addition to Monk, Tapps was also listening to Coltrane and Mingus. Altogether, these songs related stories that we couldn't hear elsewhere—crayon enlargements of life. But I can't convey how desperately we longed to claim these stories as our own without invoking the name of Henry Eagle.

Henry Eagle was our small town's most badass guy. He lived in the boys' bathroom of our high school. He didn't attend classes. You didn't see him in the hallways. He passed his youth in front of the bathroom mirror, studying, shaping, patting, and preening his hairsprayed pompadour, teasing its peak to the point of razor-cut perfection, as his transistor radio boomed "Hi-Heel Sneakers" by Tommy Tucker and "Can I Get a Witness?" by Marvin Gaye.

I was only a freshman during Henry Eagle's senior-year reign of terror, so he didn't get much of a chance to abuse me and my friends. If we recklessly strayed into the bathroom for an emergency stop, he would merely glance down at us through the cigarette haze as though observing cockroaches. Then he'd curl his upper lip and flick the two-inch ash of his filtered menthol Kools upon the tops of our high-heeled, black suede boots.

But there was one encounter with Henry Eagle that I cannot forget.

I had thoughtlessly wandered into the boys' bathroom one afternoon carrying a copy of a paperback book that Tapps had pressed upon me, *The Autobiography of Malcom X*. The book's front cover featured the famous photo of the world's most dangerous black man grimacing like a skull and extending his forefinger into the air, as though he were about to push it into the eye of white America. This affront was evident to Henry Eagle. He squinted hard at the book cover, barked a sour laugh in my face, and then he swooshed the book out of my hands and ripped it down the paper binding, dropping its two halves into the garbage bin.

"I hate niggers," he explained.

And yet everything else about Henry Eagle screamed that this could not be true.

Even now, I picture Henry Eagle as he appeared in our high school's 1964 yearbook, selected by the senior class as half of the Best Dressed couple.

Henry Eagle wore a white, French-cuffed, silk shirt with irridescent-edged pink ruffles trailing down the front like snail tracks. His tight, ash-gray, woolen trousers must have required a topographical map for successful penetration and entry. Around his waist, he fastened a scarlet cumberbund. His pale white, sheer-nylon pimp socks, discreetly peeking out from three-inch slits up the cuffs of his trousers, glistened in the reflection of the camera's flash like a bracelet of pearls strung around his ankles. Henry Eagle's impressive stature owed some debt to his four-inch platform heels stacked up under a pair of green alligator, needle-pointed, roach-killer boots. His maroon mohair jacket set off the unbuttoned black patent leather vest, which nicely complemented his three-foot walnut walking cane with a great wing-spread bird of handcarved ivory perched on the top. He wore aviator sunglasses. His too-small Stetson sat flatly, like a brick, on his mountainous razor-cut.

Standing next to him in the picture, Gloria Gertz seemed completely outclassed by the guy. Gloria wore a shoulder-to-mid-thigh black-and-white dress that looked like two flaps of plastic tablecloth. Actually, it's difficult to determine precisely what else Gloria was wearing since the angle of the photo dwells exclusively upon her huge beehive bonnet of ratted hair. She had hair like a national monument; it was widely debated whether switchblades or black widow spiders rested at its core.

Underneath the photo, the yearbook editor had inscribed this gushy tribute: Henry Eagle and Gloria Gertz—Just Like James and Aretha, meaning of course, James Brown and Aretha Franklin, two genuine heroes. Henry Eagle, who must have dreamed he was black, never had a prouder day.

~~~~~~

Everybody's upbringing is a strange country, worthy of the best anthropologists.

In her early twenties, Zora Neale Hurston began to examine her own early life from the dual perspective of an artist and academic folklorist. By night, Hurston lit up Harlem as one of the era's flashiest writers; by day, she burrowed into her textbooks at Barnard as the disciple of Franz Boas, the nation's most eminent anthropologist. To friends in either world, it was clear that Hurston was uniquely prepared to undertake a rigorous investigation into rural black folk culture of the kind that had so far eluded the field's few white professionals.

"From the earliest rocking of my cradle," Hurston recalled in her autobiography, "I had known about the capers Brer Rabbit is apt to cut and what the Squinch Owl says from the house top. But it was fitting me like a tight chemise. I couldn't see it for wearing it. It was only when I was off in college, away from my native surroundings, that I could see myself like somebody else and stand off and look at my garment. Then I had to have the spy-glass of Anthropology to look through at that."

Sometimes Hurston's aspirations rubbed each other raw, amounting to what her biographer Hemenway called "vocational schizophrenia," as literature abraded linguistic studies or the social sciences bled into storytelling. And yet there was no doubt that Hurston's early trips through the South constituted pioneering work. At the time, no American university had a folklore department. Black folklore materials were extremely limited, black collectors almost unheard of. Studies by whites often proved worse than neglect, as the researchers indulged in rhapsodic effrontery over the "primitives" they had discovered. "It makes me sick to see how these cheap white folks are grabbing our stuff and ruining it," Hurston complained, "my one consolation being that they never do it right and so there is still a chance for us."

Hurston set out to "collect like a new broom" from what she believed to be "the greatest cultural wealth of the continent." In Mobile, Alabama, she interviewed the eighty-year-old sole survivor of the last slave ship to dock upon American shores. In the Everglades, she set up a base camp and hung notices at the post office promising prizes for the "best lies" local people could recount to her. Hurston would always believe that the artist in her who could "plough up some literary and lay-by some alphabets" owed an eternal debt to the slow drawl of the front porch tongue waggers whom she had known as a child in Eatonville. For her, art had always been something that ordinary people created before they knew that Art existed.

Over several years Hurston roamed the South, collecting the stories, songs, and legends that would later fill her book *Mules and Men*. When it was published in 1935, anthropologist Alan Lomax called the work "the most engaging, genuine, and skillfully written book in the field of folklore." Years later, Alice Walker would make presents of "this perfect book!" to her family, watching them rediscover "a kind of paradise regained." Walker saw that "they could not hold back the smiles, the laughter, the *joy* over who she was showing them to be: descendants of an inventive, joyous, courageous, and outrageous people: loving drama, appreciating wit, and, most of all, relishing the pleasure of each other's loquacious and *bodacious* company." Walker herself was "soothed" by Hurston's "assurance that she was exposing not simply an adequate culture, but a superior one. That black people can be on occasion peculiar and comic was knowledge she enjoyed. That they could be racially or culturally inferior to whites never seems to have crossed her mind."

As always, music blazed the trail that Hurston was bound to follow.

"My people are not going to do but so much of anything before they sing something," Hurston once declared. Back in Eatonville, the singer had been as important a person as the storyteller—in truth, another kind of storyteller. Hurston remembered how she would tag along after the turpentine workers who passed through town, spreading their songs from one part of the South to another. "I thought they were the most exciting people in the world, stopping along, barefooted as a yard dog, playing their guitars and singing, and always the guitars had red ribbons on them."

Hurston's background provided her with credentials to which other, more experienced anthropologists eventually deferred. In New Orleans, she assisted a Columbia researcher interested in the "special" musical abilities of black people. In Florida, Hurston collected songs with Alan Lomax, who with his father had first recorded Leadbelly. Sometimes Lomax and his assistant wore blackface to avoid harassment by whites; it was Hurston's idea.

Following their experience in the Everglades, Lomax asked Hurston how she managed to accumulate her huge repertory of songs. Hurston replied:

> I just get in the crowd with the people, and if they sing it I listen as best I can and then I start to joinin' in with a phrase or two and then finally I get so I can sing a verse. And then I keep on until I learn all the verses and then I sing 'em back to the people until they tell me that I can sing 'em just like them. And then I take part and I try it out on different people who already know the song until they are quite satisfied that I know it. Then I carry it in my memory. . . . I learn the song myself and then I can take it with me whenever I go.

At one point, Hurston's commitment to black music led her to urge the Guggenheim Foundation to fund a specialized conservatory. "Imagine Duke Ellington, Fats Waller, Louis Armstrong as guest professors! Ethel Waters, Bill Robinson, etc. Can't you see the whites who have ambitions in that direction running there?"

~~~~~

I remember our band's first meeting in Tapps's garage during the fall of 1964, when we first grappled with the burden of showing who we were: white boys borrowing the black man's blues.

"How about this for a name?" suggested Space. He rose from the garage's cold cement floor where the six of us sat; he puffed perfect grey smoke ringlets from his puckered mouth. *The Shades of Silver Darkness.*

Jade East mixed with cigarette smoke and the sweat that we had worked up over a rough version of "Shout!" by the Isley Brothers. Tapps's portable transistor AM radio echoed the Sunday night dedications: To Bobby, from Susan, I swear I won't forget you, baby. And then the DJ spun "Soldier Boy," by the Shirelles.

"But what's it mean?" demanded Richie, our lead guitar player and most practical member of the band. "I mean, how can darkness be silver? If it's dark. If you get what *I* mean."

"Our name should make people respect us," proclaimed Space, ignoring Richie. "It's got to remind people of the sweet smell of success."

"I think we should name ourselves after your sweet smell," said Nick, our drummer and a hard kid. He pinched his nostrils and held his breath.

"I think we should name ourselves after your sister's smell when I'm done—"

"Shut up," said Richie, "and get serious."

Obscene, uncertain, ignorant, and inexperienced, we tended less toward civil discussion than continuous teenage-boy brawling. Even today I marvel at our adolescent crudity and quarreling, the way we nursed and pampered our obnoxious foul mouths as though they were pet snapping turtles. The only clue we had about the way the rest of the world conducted their lives came from the songs we heard on the radio. During the next summer, Watts would burn, and by the time we graduated from high school, dozens of other cities would be smouldering. We kept our ears open for any new song that could tell us why.

KYA played "Surf City" by Jan and Dean. We groaned. Nobody thought surf music could teach us a damn thing.

"What would Little Richard have called himself," wondered Space, "if he didn't already have a name and he was a group instead of one person?"

"Little Richard went to Sweden to get a sex change operation so he could marry James Brown."

"You lie."

"Truth hurts."

"It hurts when you bite my—"

"SHUT UP!" suggested Richie.

"Okay, animal names then." Tapps slipped his trumpet out of its case and spit-polished its bell with an old pair of Fruit of the Loom jockey shorts that his mom had thrown into the garage corner rag pile. "Like, you know, the Beatles."

"Four guys with Moe haircuts," said Teddy, dismissing the British white boys with a flip of his hand, "and they can't even dance."

"Okay, then, birds or something. What if we called ourselves the Orioles."

"That's taken. They did 'Crying in the Chapel.' "

"Okay. The Ravens."

"Taken."

"The Flamingos."

"Taken."

"The Cardinals."

"Taken."

"The Chicken Livers."

"It's a lame idea anyway," Richie informed us.

We stared down at the cold cement garage floor and concentrated like crazy. KYA played "Fingertips. Part 2" by Little Stevie Wonder.

"I know," said Space, his pink face brightening up like a pinball machine.

"Don't kid me, Space. What do you know?"

"Space knows lots of stuff," said Tapps, instinctively siding with the underdog. "Tell them what you know, man."

"I know the bass pattern to every major instrumental recorded since we were in fifth grade, from 'Tequila' and 'Green Onions' to 'Shotgun' and 'Harlem Nocturne.' Not to mention 'Soul Finger,' 'Wiggle Wobble,' and 'Honky Tonk, Parts One *and* Two.'"

"I should hope so," agreed Richie.

"I know that Chuck Berry used to work in a beauty parlor, Jackie Wilson boxed Golden Gloves, and the Righteous Brothers aren't even cousins."

"So tell me something *I* don't know," demanded Nick.

"I know Muddy Waters's and Howlin' Wolf's real names."

If there were ever two black men unlikely to come strolling down the sycamore streets of our stucco, tract home subdivision, with red ribbons fluttering from their guitars, they were Muddy Waters and Howlin' Wolf.

"Bullshit," argued Nick, "how do you know—"

"McKinley Morganfield and Chester Burnett." Space was gloating. "You see, I *know* that."

"My man keeps his ears open," agreed Tapps. He draped his arm around Space's skinny-kid shoulders.

"So then," demanded Nick, "what should our name be?"

Space said: the Fabulous Imitations.

Teddy stared at Space like he was a dangerous, escaped lunatic. "Man, you don't know *nothing*."

~~~~~~

When I left my New Orleans hotel room to get away from the white punk black rappers, or whatever those noisy boys next door were, I was thinking about Zora Neale Hurston's last big trip to the city in the winter of 1928–29. Hurston had arrived to burrow into the heart of Hoodoo ("or Voodoo, as pronounced by the whites"), which she said was burning like "a flame in America, with all the intensity of a suppressed religion." Far more intrepid than most literary people, Hurston aimed to get as close as possible to its core.

In New Orleans, she immersed herself in Hoodoo ritual, studying with a host of teachers and finally earning the "crown of power" through an ordeal in which she lay nude, face-down on a couch at her conjurer's house for sixty-nine hours, forgoing all food. Beneath her lay an unfurled snake skin. Hurston was never shy about getting to the heart of the story when she believed that the story was worth retelling.

As she delved deeper into the mysteries of Hoodoo, Hurston also achieved the kind of personal reconciliation that would mark her best work. New Orleans provided a vast, unobstructed view of history, in which "three hundred years of America passed like the mist of morning." For Hurston, "Africa reached out its dark hand and claimed its own." In this sense, New Orleans was as much home as Eatonville.

As I wandered back into the French Quarter around midnight, I wondered what remnants of the world Hurston had explored in the 1920s were still left in the city. In the front window of the Voodoo Museum on Dumaine Street, I found one answer in the shape of a foot-high Kewpie doll resembling David Duke, the Klansman running for governor in Louisiana. A Nazi swastika was sewn upon the doll's shoulders; he was thoroughly pierced with pins. Hoodoo was at the very least an apt jibe against the spirit of bigotry that Hurston's work had always undermined.

As both an artist and anthropologist, Hurston understood that the richness of one person—and beyond that, one culture—did not diminish another. She grasped that each part of a whole is blessed with its own resilience and integrity. She was delighted by the persistent interplay of opposing traditions—Plato (whom she studied) spinning his own form of folktale, Faulkner (who admired Hurston's work) dipping into the rhythms of the turpentine gut-bucket singers wandering from Eatonville to Yoknapatawpha County, Hurston herself tending the cacophony that rose up from the several worlds she straddled. She had the artist's capacity to revel in the ordinary; she was never ashamed of being several people at once. Henry Eagle and the rest of us could learn from her example.

I ambled through the Quarter, down Dumaine Street, up Bourbon, along Chartres, heading no place in particular. The narrow streets thronged with drunks and musicians. In Jackson Square, I rested on the cement steps to finish a bottle of beer I had carried out of a dark, noisy joint near Patout's. The moon arched above the statue of General Jackson saddled upon his horse, his hat doffed in one hand to hail the light. A boy with a trumpet stood at the foot of the invader's statue. He bleated and blahed his way through Miles Davis's "All Blues."

I slipped back into the alleyways and zigzagged for another half-hour until I found myself standing in front of Preservation Hall.

I have never been a fan of traditional jazz. Worse, I have always imagined that the traditional jazz featured inside Preservation Hall would be a shuck, like Disneyland Dixieland—an artifice, unfelt, an impersonation for the tourists. The line in front of Preservation Hall was very long, but a good tenor sax player was wandering up and down the street, playing for free, and so I took my place at the end of the line, as much to rest and listen to the sax man as gain entry. When we were finally ushered into the building, I saw that a lack of artifice was Preservation Hall's greatest asset. The hall looked about twice the size of my hotel room, dimly lit like the gloomy altar of some small country church where a few candles sputtered bravely. Six musicians sat upon wooden chairs atop a small stage raised about eighteen inches from the floor. A half-dozen wooden bench pews filed back from the stage; everybody else—maybe seventy-five people—crowded together in the darkness, shoulder to shoulder.

I didn't recognize the band's first tune, but when the trumpet player took the lead, he shaved the melody close, in the style of King Oliver. After the clarinet solo, he stood up once again and sang out to the audience. His woman had left him, giving him the blues; it was the usual story.

Traditional jazz has never seemed risky enough to me. But as the band inside Preservation Hall continued to bang out one number after another, the piano, bass, drums, banjo, clarinet, and trumpet swelling into a sea of collective fakery with sufficient spirit and peculiarity to challenge all the conventional harmonies, I caught for an inspired instant how truly daring the music must have felt at its inception. Even now the friction of creation showed sparks—the painful *hilarity* of squeezing something unheard before from a motley collection of instruments only recently transported to these shores. The band rambled on, and I realized there was nothing at all quaint about this music; it had always been full of risk, unstable, and liable to combust.

"Everyone is familiar with the Negro's modification of the whites' musical instruments," wrote Hurston in a 1931 essay "Characteristics of Negro Expression," "so that his interpretation has been adopted by the white man himself and then reinterpreted. In so many words, Paul Whiteman is giving an imitation of a Negro orchestra making use of white-invented musical instruments in a Negro way. Thus has arisen a new art in the civilized world, and thus has our so-called civilization come. The exchange and re-exchange of ideas between groups."

The bass player at Preservation Hall seemed determined to prove this point. He launched into a flutter of notes that were both too rapid and dissonant for New Orleans vintage jazz, playing more like Charles

Mingus than Pops Foster. He scurried up the instrument's neck from the bridge to the scroll, shattering the tune. The other players grunted encouragement. Together they were demonstrating how music—culture—argues, blends, dissolves, mutates, advances. The odd bird who hears something different plucks his strings too quickly or queerly or flat out plunks the *wrong* note, but he does it over and over until it sounds right. He finds his own groove and fashions new music from the old.

And that's exactly what American music—American culture—has managed to do. As Hurston understood, as the bass player was now showing, our nation's truest anthem contains the funeral dirge of the New Orleans street band combined with the whorehouse piano and the last slave's work song and the bickering melodies of two hundred disparate points of origin, from Marseilles to Dakar, from Manaus to Guangzhou, now stretched out over the American plains like the hide of some mythical beast: the confluence of influences that nobody will ever be able to pick apart note-for-note. It has long been a sophisticated complaint to jeer that America has "no culture," but there couldn't be a sillier idea. We have more culture than one people will ever be able to digest. And that helps explain why the melting pot sometimes bubbles up—and when we least expect it, explodes.

~~~~~

I remember the spotlight gleaming.

Some of the guys wore shades on stage. I always stared out into the audience and watched the sea of dancing bodies: the waves of indistinct, bobbing faces that whooped, screamed, and sang along to the three-chord melodies that we all knew by heart.

To begin the evening, Tapps and I would wrap our lips around the cold metal mouthpieces of our trumpet and sax to blow the top two notes of a hard, flat C-minor seventh.

Along with Richie, our guitar player, we'd hit the chord four times in succession. Then Teddy would flit out from stage left, skating across the floor on the edge of one white patent leather boot. When he reached the microphone set center stage, he'd pull the stand into his chest like it was the most beautiful skinny girl in the world. You could see his mouth watering.

Desire.

Teddy Chavez could duckwalk like Chuck Berry and sing the full vocal range of Sam and Dave. He pranced around the stage, constantly jiggling and bobbing his hands, knees, head, and feet—in perpetual motion like all five of the Temptations. In the middle of the stage, the spotlight reflecting off his lacquered smile, he danced the Jerk, Swim, Mashed Potato, Hully Gully, Monkey, Pony, Camel Walk, Funky Chicken, Fly, Boogaloo, Shing-a-ling, Locomotion, Twist, and Watusi. Teddy Chavez was a master of falsetto, a scholar of the splits.

"If you leave me—" sang Teddy.

Drumroll . . .

"If you leave me—"

Staccato punctuation by the horns . . .

"If you leave me—"

Nothing but silence across the dance floor at Carpenter's Hall . . .

". . . I'LL GO CRAZY . . ."

We always opened with "I'll Go Crazy," and it's still one of my favorite James Brown songs. We played them all. We studied the album *James Brown and His Famous Flames Live at the Apollo, Volumes I and II* as though it were scripture. Our own stage show was a masterpiece of imitation. We even did the James Brown bit with the cape. Teddy fell to the floor on his spaghetti legs, while Tapps covered him with a purple velvet cape and tried to persuade him to pull his weary self offstage. Teddy kept running back for more, breaking into "Please, Please, Please."

I never thought for a moment that we were ripping off the music. Rather, I think we were all very thankful to have learned these songs as young as we did.

But just in case, I want to thank James Brown, once again, right now. Thank you, James Brown, for "Please, Please, Please," and "I'll Go Crazy." Thank you, Godfather of Soul, Mr. Dynamite, Mr. T.N.T., for "I Got the Feeling," "You Got the Power," and "I Got You." Thank you, Hardest Working Man in Show Business, for "Cold Sweat," "Night Train," "There Was a Time," "Try Me," and "Ain't That a Groove." Thank you, James, for "Lost Someone," "Papa's Got a Brand New Bag," "Let Yourself Go," "It's a Man's, Man's, Man's World," and "Money Won't Change You (But Time Will Take You Out)."

Thank you, James Brown, for the inspiration.

The music that we felt most deeply as kids rose up from the roots of this country. From black people, most essentially, most heroically and gorgeously, of course; but also, somehow, from other parts of the heartland where it was later translated, reformed, diluted, renewed. The best of our American music has always been soulful in all the bright and sad ways of ordinary lives.

But to whom, exactly, does James Brown—or for that matter, Zora Neale Hurston—belong?

Certainly, they both belong to America's black people; but not exclusively, no more than Mozart's operas or Leadbelly's blues can be the property of one people, even one nation. James Brown and Zora Neale Hurston are *American* geniuses. And for that, they deserve our wider appreciation.

I should also take a moment *right now* to thank Sam and Dave on TV's Monday night "Shindig." And Smokey Robinson and Marvin Gaye on Thursday night's "Hullabaloo." Thank you for the 45s from Duke, Peacock, Chess, Stax, Volt, Atlantic, and Motown. Otis Redding singing

"Fa, Fa, Fa, Fa, Fa, Fa, Fa, Fa, Fa" (*You sing it now!*) and "Dock of the Bay." Bobby Blue Bland pitying the fool and turning on his lovelight. Junior Walker's screaming sax on "Shotgun." Solomon Burke teaching the Rolling Stones about everybody needing somebody to love. Wilson Pickett, Wicked Pickett, Mr. Funky Broadway, who knew that Ninety-Nine and a Half just wouldn't do (*he had to have one hundred!*), who told us Don't Fight It (Do It!), who took Mustang Sally to the Land of 1,000 Dances and who will always be remembered In the Midnight Hour. And Mr. Arthur Conley, wrapping up the entire story in "Sweet Soul Music."

I still think that James Brown said it best.

"I'm not going to sing this song for myself now," the Godfather of Soul confided to his audiences at the Apollo, "I'm singing it for you too."

James Brown was singing it for us too twenty years ago when Richie D'Vinio's father stumbled mean drunk into one of our rehearsals on a Saturday afternoon and wanted to beat the hell out of us all.

Richie, Tapps, and I were working out some dance steps for the band in the privacy of Richie's bedroom. Despite the summer heat, we were wearing our white ruffled stage shirts just to set the mood. We drew the window shades. Richie's desk lamp shone upon us like a spotlight.

Naturally, the record player was blasting.

That's when Richie's dad walked into the bedroom and hollered about how much he hated the song that we had been playing over and over and over on Richie's phonograph for the past two hours. The song was the Ray Charles righteous LP version of "I Believe to My Soul."

"Christ, look at you three," bellowed Richie's dad. "Like a bunch of god damn fairies prancing around here like that."

"It's okay, Dad," said Richie. He could see that the old man had been drinking.

"Makes me sick. *Who do you think you are?* Turn down that god damned jungle music."

"It's *okay,* Dad. We'll turn it down."

"Turn it down? The hell you're going to turn it down. I'm going to throw that god damn record out the window."

Chub D'Vinio hauled himself across the room toward the record player. He was a big man, thick muscles slabbed together like a side of beef. He was very menacing and he was very drunk.

"That's my record," I told him, "so don't touch it."

Chub D'Vinio wheezed with exasperation, and then he stared very hard at me, not believing what had sprouted up under his nose.

I was growing a beard. It was summer, and there was no school dress code to worry about. My beard was fuzzy, sparse, and precisely trimmed. I thought I looked slick and devil-may-care, but Chub D'Vinio did not agree.

He knocked me down, pushed me flat to the ground, and then he was on top of me and all over me, both hands pulling at my face.

"Who do you think you are?" he demanded. He tried to pluck my beard out of my chin, tugging away at the roots. "WHO DO YOU THINK YOU ARE?" he roared into my face.

Richie wrapped an arm around his throat from behind, trying to pull him off.

"Get off, Dad, he didn't mean it."

Tapps turned up the music on the phonograph.

Ray Charles's "I Believe to My Soul" was blasting from both speakers.

"Get off him, Dad!"

Tapps turned the music up as loud as it would go.

"GET OFF!"

Chub must have weighed 250 pounds, even more when he was sloppy drunk, but he flitted off me suddenly like a butterfly and floated down the hall. I could hear the screen door slam, and his car start up, and then he peeled out down the street.

I crawled up onto my feet. Strangely enough, I was thinking about the weekend before, when I'd come to pick up Richie for a gig. His mom and dad were dancing in their living room with the shades pulled tight and the lights dimmed. On the phonograph, Frank Sinatra crooned "Witchcraft." Chub had been seriously drunk that night too, but it had been a happy drunk. He told me that "Sinatra was still the god damned best," and that I should tell that to everybody in our band. I thought he was a fool.

Now Tapps, Richie, and I stood in the bedroom with the record player blasting "I Believe to My Soul" by Ray Charles.

We were embarrassed. We didn't know what to say to each other.

"I oughta kill that guy," mumbled Richie.

"Don't say that, man," said Tapps, "he's your dad."

"You okay?" Richie asked me.

"Yeah."

"He didn't mean it, man."

"Yeah."

But what did he mean?

I know that Chub didn't like my beard. And I *had* challenged him. He was drunk. And I suspect the sight of three teenage boys, decked out in ruffled shirts and dancing together in the dark, could have easily set him off.

But most of all, just like he said, Chub D'Vinio hated the song we were playing.

Who *did* we think we were?

Richie's dad loathed the fact that we believed Ray Charles and James Brown had more to teach us than he ever would. He heard in the music the same message that Henry Eagle had read on the cover of *The Auto-biography of Malcolm X*; it was the same truth that Zora Neale Hurston had engraved into the national literature, the same sound that drove me out of my New Orleans hotel room: despite fear and mistrust, the squirming parts of the American whole cannot help rubbing up against each other and changing each other, usually for the better. We cannot help becoming each other's heroes.

Richie's old man, Henry Eagle, all of us, at some point, presume that our culture is unified by one voice: our own. But America is the world's most blaring, off-key, hand-clapping choir. You can hear the choir every day on Dumaine Street in New Orleans, or in San Francisco's Mission District, or on the South Side of Chicago—you can even hear its echo in Boise, Missoula, and Fargo, North Dakota.

TURN UP THE MUSIC!

"MOOSE. . . MAINE. . . THOREAU. . ."

I am reminded by my journey how
exceedingly new this country still is.

—Henry David Thoreau, *The Maine Woods*

From the beginning, Ann and I had planned to delve into the Maine Woods, like Thoreau, for the moose.

I had never seen one.

Moose, to me, was Bullwinkle. Or the bottle label on Canadian beer. Or the poor heads hung in taverns from Sitka, Alaska, to Halifax, Nova Scotia. Yet the moose in reality—in the wild—is an unforgettable fellow.

Thoreau called the moose "God's own horses," noting that the fabulous creatures would have required invention as a shadowy presence in the forest had they not already shown the good grace to exist. The author proclaimed in *The Maine Woods*, his book covering three expeditions into the wilds of Maine during 1846, 1853, and 1857, that he was equally concerned with the moose as with the trees. And as every Thoreau enthusiast knows, the last comprehensible utterance to pass the dying writer's lips was: Moose . . . Indian . . . .

For years I had longed to see the mighty, gangly moose, King Ridiculous of the Forest, blithely clunking his was through murky preserves. In recent days, this whim had become a fixation. For six months, I had been traveling in a dozen states, hopping from identical airport to indistinguishable motel in countless homogenized communities from coast to coast. In many places—most places—it seemed as though the last remnants of parochial distinction had been bulldozed and paved to make room for the new mall at the air-conditioned edge of town where the blanding of America appeared almost complete. The country was lurching toward permanent convenience. And it made me sad to recognize what had vanished from sight: the local quirks and rough edges, the accumulated national crankiness that had given our country shape and character.

I needed to look into the face of something wild. A moose would suit me fine.

But it wasn't just any moose I was seeking; I wanted Thoreau's moose. And I wasn't interested in the stay-at-home Thoreau who hovered cozily upon the banks of Walden pond, but rather, the rank and wooly Thoreau, a weather-beaten explorer of Maine's wilderness.

The Thoreau Ann and I enrolled as our guide through the Maine Woods had declared himself "a mystic, a transcendentalist, and a natural philosopher to boot." He might have also added that he was an unapologetic idler, an erratic misanthrope, and the model for much hearty and fatuous national eccentricity that would follow; he is still our greatest crank. And he was the first to publicly dread the blanding of America in spirit, design, and policy.

In fact, Thoreau's biography seems largely a resume of repudiations and misgivings regarding the "desperate odd-fellow society" that he forever longed to escape. He neither married nor maintained a passionate liaison; he didn't vote or attend church. When his transcendental comrades asked him to join the party at Brook Farm, he snapped that he would "rather keep a bachelor's hall in hell than go to board in heaven." (The utopian communities, he believed, had "not associated, they have only assembled.") Even his friends (and friends to Thoreau were as crucial as solitude) frequently couldn't puzzle out the essential motives behind this retreat. "I have never been able to understand what he meant by his life," admitted Ellery Channing, perhaps the writer's closest friend. Thoreau was "always manly and able, but rarely tender," complained Emerson, his mentor, "as if he did not feel himself except in opposition."

And yet, admitted Emerson, "no truer American existed."

To me, these credentials added up beautifully. I wanted to get *away:* far from the city, where I could gaze into the face of some great hulking beast whose obsidian pupils were still swollen to the size of golf balls when the first morning light glinted hard off the lake. From this snout-to-nose encounter, I might escape from the rampaging sameness that was flattening the nation. And so Ann and I headed straight to the heart of central Maine, where we expected to locate both the soul of Thoreau and the spectacle of his moose.

We left Mount Desert Island after camping along the rocky shore for a week, slipped past the tourist atrocities of Bar Harbor, beyond the blur of minimarts, T-shirt shoppes, and frozen yogurt franchises that made up the small town roadside attractions of Ellsworth, Brewer, Orland, and Milford. We figured ourselves lucky to be able to so quickly flee the kind of future that Thoreau's life had been hard set against. ("What is the nature of the luxury which enervates and destroys nations?" Thoreau had asked—and the advertisements of $3.99 lobster sandwiches gleaming from the golden arches of central Maine's McDonald's answered him eloquently.) Toward Millinocket, the going got better. We rounded Baxter State Park, 201,018 expeditionary acres founded upon the philanthropic thunder of former Maine governor Percival Proctor Baxter, who as a boy had read Thoreau's accounts of Maine and set about buying up land in the 1930s from the railroads and timber companies. Then we dropped down into the state's thick, low-lying woods surrounding the Chesuncook River.

Off the main roads, the region's dense forests outlined a liquid squiggle of rivers and lakes, and the surrounding land proved as richly boggy as a swamp. ("It is all mossy and *moosey*," explained Thoreau in *The Maine Woods*.) Fronted by dense stands of slim and elegant white and yellow birch, the forest bristled, flushed out on the sides by spruce, hemlock, cedar, and pine. "The trees are a *standing* night," the writer observed, "and every fir and spruce which you fell is a plume plucked from night's raven wing. Then at night the general stillness is more impressive than any sound, but occasionally you hear the note of an owl farther or nearer in the woods, and if near a lake, the semi-human cry of the loons at their unearthly revels."

The Maine woods teem with secret lives.

Among them, there must be moose.

The moose is the world's largest antlered animal. He descends from prehistoric ancestors whose chestnut shovel of horns might have scooped up and carried about several squirming Neanderthals. He's the tallest mammal on the continent, standing up to six and a half feet at the shoulder and stretching more than ten feet long; the moose ranks a close second to the bison as the heaviest North American herbivore, weighing in between seven and thirteen hundred pounds. He should be easy to find.

We had been instructed to seek him at the source—which is to say any forest stream, lake, river, or pond—toward dawn or dusk. Athletic morning or moonlight swimmers, moose can paddle along steadily at six miles per hour, covering fifteen miles at a time. (That barrel torso also contains huge lungs; the moose can dunk his head, lower his metabolic rate, and stay submerged for four minutes.) Yet apart from the plaques of decapitated heads and the antler bouquets that bloom from the restaurant walls of central Maine in gruesome abundance, the moose managed to elude us for days.

In fact, the wildest thing we found in all of Baxter State Park was a turkey.

We had been tramping over the thick brush that seasonally splays across the park's meandering trails when a distraught wild turkey hen thrust herself out from the scrub into the air, wobbled over our heads in a dithering arc, and dropped at our feet like a feathery six-pound cannon shot. She squalled, squawked, flitted, flapped, and fanned her tail feathers with bird-brained pique, as though we had awakened her from pleasant nesting dreams of grubs and beetles. Her beady eyes flashed above her gibbering beak in an expression of indignation and astonishment; but they were not the wild eyes I longed to see.

On another afternoon, we wandered along the isolated shore of some nameless pond and stumbled upon a procession of beaver tracks that pointed the way to an elaborate masterpiece of woody wreckage blocking the water's flow. The dam promised much buck-toothed chomping and busy tail-paddling later in the evening, but though we sat there for two hours, no beaver turned up. Instead, we reclined upon a mat of leaves and twigs and watched an eddy ripple into a dozen variegated hues, the cold-water plaits of silver and gray twining into the pond's sunset weave of fading, oily blue. At one moment, the still water seemed to launch itself into a shimmering frenzy, its surface of light perversely imitating the static broadcast of a black-and-white television set.

Silence is another world. And for a long moment, we forgot about ourselves, about the creatures we had been looking for, about any vestige of the air-conditioned dread that we might have carried with us into the woods. Instead, we directed our attention to the motionless stump of pine on the shore and the graying patch of blue above—until the sudden four-footed thrashing about of rabbits or mice in the brush woke us to the world around us, and we remembered that we better head back to our camp before dark.

Still no moose, but the great pleasure of searching for him placed us as far as possible from our ordinary lives.

Thoreau had also struck out for Maine as a respite from the ordinary, though in his case, it meant the twenty-six-month residency at Walden. He had had enough of civilization, even at the distance afforded by his ten-by-fifteen-foot cabin where he lived alone alongside the eponymous pond and inveigled "the earth to say beans instead of grass" while wrestling with the first versions of his masterpiece. In Maine, Thoreau took a break from "blissful, innocent nature," which was, by the writer's lights, just about every out-of-doors place he had seen *but* Maine. When Thoreau ascended the gale-blown crags of Mount Katahdin, the state's mile-high pinnacle at the southern tip of Baxter State Park, he recognized that the frightful landscape was "made out of Chaos and Old Night. Here," he admitted, "was no man's garden."

Wildness always involves risk, and the Maine expeditions were incomparably more dangerous than garden life at Walden. The writer bore up under storms, forded high waters, scaled mountains, paddled rivers, and got himself terrifyingly lost. All this is recorded in *The Maine Woods* with less studious detail than is lavished upon the desiccated economies of *Walden*. The former book's style is more pepper and dash, probably because the landscape demanded a different way of working.

In Maine, Thoreau was at last far from his desk, traveling hard, scribbling notes amid persistent observation; then when he got home, he would quickly work up his sensory impressions and field data into a full-blown piece, revising over time. But not for one moment did Thoreau consider relinquishing his vantage at the edge of Concord society to establish himself for good amid the truly wild woods. "For a permanent residence," he wrote, "it seems to me there could be no comparison between [Walden] and the wilderness, necessary as the latter is for a resource and a background, the raw material of all our civilization."

That's a remarkable admission for the man we have come to regard as America's first spokesman for nature. Yet much of Thoreau's greatness is tied to his boundless talent for contradiction. The dreamiest of men was also the most disciplined. If he boasted about his need for a daily four-hour walk in the woods, he was more coy about the equal number of morning hours spent writing the endless journals, revising the books that nobody bought. He was a poet; but he also appeared naturally mathematical and mechanical, earning a reputation as an excellent surveyor and providing numerous technical innovations that caused his family's pencil-manufacturing business to prosper.

And yet Thoreau did not take pride in the practical side of his nature.

"Our thoughts are the epochs of our lives," he insisted, "all else is but as a journal of the winds that blew while we were here."

~~~~~

We traveled to Moosehead Lake, which sounded ideal for the task of locating a moose. The local Penobscot Indians used to call Moosehead Lake *Mspame* or "large water," and although you can't see, hear, or smell the twelve-mile-wide, thirty-mile-long lake even fifty yards from its thickly wooded shore, you can *feel* its presence with every step. Moosehead Lake seems an essential part of the surrounding forest, an anchor whose weight of distinction separates this part of the woods from the ocean of wilderness that rolls on for hundreds of miles in three directions. In *The Maine Woods*, Thoreau described Moosehead Lake as "a suitably wild-looking sheet of water, sprinkled with small, low islands, which were covered with shaggy spruce and other wild wood." Not much has changed.

On our first evening, we listened to the eerie cry of loons on the shoreline. The woods were wrapped around the lake's perimeter like a fortress of dark stanchions. The world beyond seemed a mere squint in the dark. As the moon rose to its full height, the reflection spilled across the water's surface like a vast milk slick, and I could feel the lonely distance that we had traveled, all to gaze into the face of something wild.

The next morning, we settled back down to our task. Since we were now admitting to ourselves that we probably weren't capable of locating a moose on our own, Ann thought it logical for us to seek help. And yet from the beginning, I had been shy about consulting with the locals.

The Central Mainers seemed an odd, unapproachable lot, whose rural gothic sensibility repelled casual intimacy. Their puggish Scots-Irish-English faces and physiques brought to mind Appalachia. They seemed more indebted to Hawthorne than Thoreau.

And yet all this rural gothic reticence, clannishness, suspicion, and monosyllabic hesitation vanished the moment we approached the man whom everybody along the lake acknowledged to be the local expert; and we bravely confronted him with this magic word: *Moose.*

Within seconds, we were sitting down over brackish, warmed-up cups of coffee for an hour-and-a-half disquisition on moose, their mating habits, their antlers, the uproarious drizzle that sounded from their muzzles when they were extracted from the water (this leaky racket is the surest way for woodsmen to locate the animals feeding near shore), and finally, the time of year when hunters could apply for permits to shoot them.

"The season lasts six days," explained our moose expert. "They pick a thousand people. That's it. Lottery."

"Have you ever applied?" asked Ann.

"Yep."

"Ever won?"

"Nope."

"But would you really want to shoot a moose?" she insisted.

Our moose expert thought it over. He refilled his coffee cup, then hers, then mine.

A long, inscrutable moment of Central Mainer rural gothic deliberation. . . .

"Maybe."

I'm certain that we got the royal moose treatment from the resident expert because moose are something about which many Mainers can feel proud in the same way that some westerners swell up with self-regard over the existence of the Rocky Mountains or the Pacific Ocean. And yet this pride—of what? . . . ownership? proximity?—doesn't stop people from mowing down the mountains in favor of ski resorts, scattering condos up and down the coast, or shooting moose during a six-day season. Even Thoreau got confused on this score.

On his second trip to Maine, in 1853, Thoreau enrolled as the peripheral accomplice to a moose hunt, "a chaplain or reporter" trailing along after his Indian guide, who was unabashedly out after moose meat. Having listened to tribal myths about the first moose rising from the sea, a kind of whale with guts of jellyfish, Thoreau "wished to see a moose near at hand, and was not sorry to learn how the Indian managed to kill one."

As the party stumbled upon their first moose in the woods, the practical naturalist in the writer took command, and Thoreau found himself furiously noting taxonomical distinctions. "The moose is singularly grotesque and awkward to look at," he observed. "Why should it stand so high at the shoulders? Why have so long a head? Why have no tail to speak of?"

Moments later the fabulous, hulking creature lay bleeding on the ground, felled by the Indian's rifle. Thoreau was a hunter himself, but the dead moose disturbed him. That night he joined in eating the fried meat over the campfire, thinking it something close to veal. But he was also relieved to limit the expedition's prey to a solitary cow, believing that "one moose killed was as good, if not as bad, as a dozen. The afternoon's tragedy, and my share in it, as it affected the innocence, destroyed the pleasure of my adventure."

It wasn't long before Thoreau moved from talking about the "tragedy" to "the murder of the moose." And by the end of the trip, when his party came upon a band of Indians who had slaughtered twenty-two moose in two months, taking only the skins and a small amount of meat and leaving the carcasses to rot on the ground, the writer's revulsion could not be contained. This mass murder of the moose seemed too close to swaggering out into a neighbor's pasture to shoot his horses. "Altogether," declared Thoreau, "it was about as savage a sight as was ever witnessed, and I was carried back at once three hundred years."

For weeks after returning to Walden, Thoreau felt sullied by his Maine experience, "coarser" for his part in the moose's downfall. "Every creature is better alive than dead," Thoreau believed, "men and moose and pine trees, and he who understands it aright will rather preserve its life than destroy it." Yet by his own account, he was profitably reminded, with a conviction that even now seems too blunt and earnest to qualify as sentimentality, "that our life should be lived as tenderly and daintily as one would pluck a flower."

~~~~~~

The best advice didn't produce a moose.

According to our resident expert, the beasts infested virtually every mossy, moosey inlet, island, swamp, shoreline, and densely wooded shore; basically, as Moosehead Lake's name implies, moose were everywhere.

Yet for five days running, they eluded us with quadruped cunning at every pond and glade.

And reading Thoreau only reminded me of the loss.

"Think of our life in nature," Thoreau had rhapsodized, "daily to be shown matter, to come in contact with it—rocks, trees, wind on our cheeks! the *solid* earth! the *actual* world! the *common sense*! *Contact! Contact! Who* are we? *Where* are we?"

We were idling in Maine without moose. Diminished by their absence. Silly from looking. And it was already the Fourth of July, the nation's 215th birthday, nearly our last day before we had to leave Maine and head home.

We got an early start that morning at sunrise. In the evening we planned to celebrate Independence Day in Greenville, the closest town to Moosehead Lake. Fourteen hours left to locate a moose.

We weaved back and forth from the lake's perimeter into the surrounding woods, inspecting every swamp and shore. Several times we picked up their huge hoof prints, which always led straight into the water and then vanished. Once Ann thought she spotted a young cow standing at attention in the forest, but it turned out to be a stump of dead spruce. Occasionally I mistook the chatter of crows for the clash of antlers.

In the very late afternoon, exhausted and discouraged, we decided to split up. Ann kept a silent vigil on the lake, while I veered off upon some looping spaghetti trails engraved with heavy tracks that definitely looked to me like moose or else some other equivalently lumbering, fey beast. I quickened my pace, vowing not to lift my eyes from the forest floor until I found the creature at the other end of the tracks. In ten minutes, I found myself profoundly lost.

"Ann!" I cried out sharply, "Ann, where are you?"

Her sweet voice sounded about thirty yards away.

"Don't worry, I'm right here."

I peered through a darkening stand of white speckled birch in the direction of her voice, realizing that the tracks I had been following were engraved by our own lumbering, fey feet whose bootprints had been obscured in the muck; I retraced our original path back to the lake's shore.

"Honey," she asked, "why'd you come back so soon?"

I thought quickly. "Just checking to see if you're okay."

"Well, I'm fine."

"Well then, good. I guess I better go a little deeper into the forest now."

"That'd be fine, too. Just watch out."

Well, of course I would watch out. Watching out was what we had come to Maine to do. I plodded along a snaky trail turned soggy from one of the fifteen-minute storms that blew over Moosehead Lake several times each day. After nearly thirty minutes of trudging, I recognized that I was probably once again lost, but this time it didn't really worry me. I knew *they* were out there. The sun dipped below the tree line and the lake receded behind the final glow of the forest. I pursued the soggy trail like the brave moose itself. As I wound my path through clumps of pine and birch, pungent odors rose up from the muck-brown floor— less mossy and moosey than murky and mucousy. I slowed my pace, cautiously measuring the weight of each step upon the yielding ground.

And then with one great astonishing mismeasure of myself, I plunged into a bog.

My right leg submerged into the slime and goo—"the *solid* earth! the *actual* world!"—and I sank up to my thigh. Attempting to gain purchase, I quickly pivoted my other leg toward the edge of the trail, slammed my dangling boot against what appeared to be hardened crust, but wasn't, and sunk my left thigh up to a corresponding level of muck.

I squirmed about manfully for a good minute or two.

And then I sank up to my crotch.

"Ann?" I called out, stupidly calm, to the empty woods.

No answer.

"Ann!" I repeated more emphatically to the birch and pine trees enclosing the bog; and then, in a panic, to anyone: "*Help!*"

The sun had begun to set, which is a good time for spotting not only moose but mosquitoes. A profusion of mosquitoes wafted toward me like a black cloud as I slowly subsided another fraction of an inch into the center of the earth.

"SOMEBODY, HELP ME!"

Soon they were upon me, these lonely creatures of the forest, these wild beasts with pinpoint faces too minute to gaze into, buzzing and lighting upon my neck, hands, and arms. A bog in Maine is no place to be stuck at sunset. A stench recalling several million years of primordial putrescence bubbled up from the deeper recesses whenever I wiggled my feet and thighs. I slipped another inch into the goo, and I thought about dying.

Picture this: I was alone, confused, covered with a blanket of mosquitoes, feeling absurd, fearing I might die—but I couldn't help thinking that at least I wasn't stuck in some nameless indistinguishable motel room in yet another homogenized city; this place in which I was immersed had nothing to do with the blanding of America, the paved-over nation. I was really out in the wild.

And these thoughts actually calmed me. Instead of thrashing about and corkscrewing myself deeper into the mire, I relaxed. And I soon

found that if I didn't struggle, I didn't sink. I had oozed into a *metaphor.*
In fact, it seemed that I had hit bottom.

Exhausted, ridiculous, immobilized, but relieved by the probability
that I wouldn't descend further into the bog and entirely disappear, I
closed my eyes for a moment, watched my eyelids flicker with fatigue,
and then dropped off into dreamless sleep for an immeasurable instant.

That's when I heard the moose.

Some gigantic commotion resounded in the woods, startling me
awake; then I perceived its rollicking, clamorous lope through the
nearby bramble. I imagined a huge bull moose quickening home to his
lair, cutting through the bog, and then suddenly—*stumbling upon me*!

I was being charged by an angry moose!

I'd only wanted to take a peek at the creature. I'd merely longed for
contact, as Thoreau had recommended.

The clamor intensified, the beast crashing and stomping through the
brush, nine hundred pounds of enraged antlers.

And then, in an instant, the moose was upon me.

The bramble and high shrubs surrounding the bog were breached
with a frenzied crash, and before I could even see the beast, I could hear
it snorting, wheezing, bellowing at me angrily, windily, horribly. He
sounded like a terrible creature, and yet when I caught my first glimpse
of the moose I'd been seeking for days, he turned out to be shorter
than I had imagined—and thinner, with blonde curls bouncing upon
his shoulders, and he was wearing (this is the oddest part) blue jeans
and a bright-red down vest. He was calling out my name, and laughing,
and then clapping his hooves together, extending a pointed index finger
at me while exclaiming rapturously that I looked like a glassy-bald tire
that somebody had inserted into the muck, like some prehistoric artifact
gleaming in the slime. I was waist-deep in filth, and he was laughing
uncontrollably. In fact, the moose was Ann.

~~~~~~

Thoreau (as Orwell said of Dickens) is a writer worth stealing, and every side gets a hand upon him at some point.

For my money, the most egregious theft was committed by the Reagan camp in the 1980s when they expropriated the Thoreauvian phrase it's "morning in America," even as the nation descended into its deepest slumber in decades, and politics became a dreadful sleepwalk.

"To be awake is to be alive," insisted Thoreau, who suffered from a mild case of narcolepsy and knew firsthand the dangers of dropping off in the midst of things. "I have never yet met a man who was quite awake."

When Ann, instead of a charging bull moose, arrived at my bog, I was feeling more awake than I had ever felt in my life. After I explained how I had come to be stewing there, she stopped laughing and lowered an overhanging pine branch into reach. I arched upwards, clasped the branch with two hands, and extricated myself with a single pull-up.

We headed back to camp, where I changed into some clean clothes; then we hopped into our car and sped down the two-lane country road to Greenville, where much of the county collected around Moosehead Lake would be celebrating Independence Day.

We were too late for everything except the fireworks.

Over the water, the rockets and roman candles burst low and luxuriously, unraveling like spiderwebs above the crowd of four- or five-hundred people. Almost the entire town had bunched up on the shore, and they clapped, panted, and cried out ecstatically with each explosion. For almost an hour, the display illuminated the horizon, and then the last rocket sped across the sky, flaring with a sudden, promising, bright burst—and then nothing. It was the first Independence Day following the war with Iraq, and the country, as Emerson had complained of Thoreau, was feeling itself entirely in opposition. It was easy enough to say who our nation now stood against, but still quite mysterious as to what we stood for. American flags fluttered upon jacket lapels and blouses; they waved from scores of radio aerials on Ford pickup trucks and family Buicks, flying from the ramparts of convenience stores and patriotic hamburger joints. Days before, at a small department store downtown, we had discovered a lavish window display in which the Arabian desert battle was reenacted by green plastic toy soldiers and model airplanes, the final slaughter calling to mind horses gunned down in some neighbor's sandy pasture.

All this, combined with my evening in the bog and our days of failing to locate even a solitary moose, depressed me deeply.

Perhaps it wasn't fair, but the whole laundry list of grievances soon came pouring out: once again I was reminded that it wasn't morning in America, but a much darker time. Even Maine, proud home of the nation's most self-conscious odd ducks, was beginning to mall itself over in a feat of pointless impersonation, one place (Ellsworth, or Brewer, or Orland, or Greenville) looking like any place else. Maine might still contain some of the nation's wildest country, but much of the state that was no longer wild now seemed as bland as an egg. The desperate enthusiasm for a war that would have sickened Maine's most celebrated visitor seemed just another way of stating the problem.

Thoreau's first trip to Maine had come just a few weeks after the night he spent in Concord's jail—the source of his essay "Civil Disobedience." Thoreau was protesting the poll tax maintained to fuel President Polk's war in the Far West with Mexico, which would eventually cede to the nation Texas, Arizona, New Mexico, California, and portions of Colorado and Wyoming. For his part, Thoreau had always been a partisan of westering. But the West in the imagination of this inveterate Easterner chiefly existed as a metaphor—like my bog before it became *too* real. When Thoreau urged the nation toward the Pacific, he was actually advocating a journey down deep inside, to untamed places. He believed that a trip to the wilds should lead to the essentials, not reckless diversions like imperialist war.

Here's one more of the great writer's contradictions: as the most apolitical of the transcendentalists (who were not, as popularly presumed, navel-gazers and absentminded idealists, but rather staunch reformers of every progressive stripe, from abolition to woman's suffrage), Thoreau had the most lasting effect of the bunch upon the political culture of our nation, even the world. Thoreau's ideas, spurred on by classical eastern philosophy, quickly circled back to their beginnings, circumnavigating the globe to meet the young Gandhi in South Africa, Tolstoy in Russia, Martin Luther King in our own country and century.

For all his peevishness toward society and enthusiasm for the individual, Thoreau was too good a naturalist, too shrewd an ecologist, to believe in the self-sufficiency of a single organism. He knew himself first to be an essential cell of his own family, then a link in the chain of a small circle of friends; even, despite the famous objections, the spawn of a larger pond called Concord. Somewhere between Concord and the cosmos lay his allegiance to America, and he could never regard the country blandly.

"I trust that we shall be more imaginative," Thoreau had written, "that our thoughts will be clearer, fresher, and more ethereal, as our sky—our understanding more comprehensive and broader, like our plains . . . and our hearts shall even correspond in breadth and depth and grandeur to our inland seas. . . . Else to what end does the world go on, and why was America discovered?"

As the fireworks ended, Ann wandered off toward the concession stands to purchase our dinner of beer and nachos. The last clouds of citizens dispersed like mosquitoes. We climbed into our car and proceeded back to our camp on the two-lane road. The path was dark and silent, our disappointment as heavy as the late evening fog settling upon the lake. As we drove back to our camp, we admitted aloud that we had failed, that our opportunities were now exhausted. The road wound into the woods and the lights of Greenville vanished with a sudden curve. In six hours, we would be flying back to California. We had not managed to look into the face of the wild beast, and now it was time to leave.

Then in the corner of our high-beams, we caught the sight of some huge hulking shape mounted above a roadside pond.

"What was it?"

"You know," said Ann.

Thoreau had once written that "genius is a light which makes the darkness visible, like the lightning's flash." Our moose had presented himself to us along the midnight road with the same rapidity and dazzle.

We turned around and parked against a dense stand of birch. The moose held his ground at the pond, ignoring us. He stood about seven feet high, his antlers spread out in the moonlight like huge wooden wings, his black leather ears twitching and flapping at the circle of flies that buzzed around his shoulders like a necklace. We padded up close, maybe ten yards away. In the glow of the moon, I could see how his ridiculous muzzle tapered into his snout, and how the indented lines of his long, straight jaw drew his mouth into the characteristic moose pucker so that he appeared to be grinning. His entire body was reflected in the motionless surface of the moonlit pond so that two moose appeared to be standing before us—one staring directly at us with his ironic smile, the other shimmering across the flat water.

And then he skidded off. Two lopes and he was into the woods. And we'd lost him.

Ann and I moved closer together, silently creeping up to the edge of the pond. We stared into the forest where our solitary moose had flashed off like lightning. And I outrageously hoped for a desperate instant that there might always be one more chance for the wild, stubborn genius of the unpaved nation.

MY FATHER'S
JACK LONDON

You can go anywhere out through the Golden Gate—to
Australia, to Africa, to the seal islands, to the North Pole, to
Cape Horn. . . . Oakland's just a place to start from, I guess.
—Jack London, *Valley of the Moon*

Dad and I met at the gangplank to board the San Francisco ferry at Oakland's Jack London Square.

"You sure you don't have to work today?" asked my father. "I don't want to take you away from work."

"Really," I assured him, "I can take the day off."

"Well, work all you can," he lectured me, far from the first time, "work long and hard, because 'Life is real! Life is earnest! And the grave—' "

"I know, 'the grave is not its goal,' is it?"

"Longfellow," he pointed out.

"Right."

Morning commuters swelled behind us, scuffling their shoes upon the sandpaper footholds, clattering their briefcases against the iron handrail.

"Aren't there any working people on this boat?" my father asked incredulously, glaring down the gangplank. Dad hadn't crossed the bay on the early morning ferry since the 1930s, when he commuted from San Francisco's port to the Alameda Naval Air Base, where he was to work as a metalsmith for thirty-seven years.

"It looks to me like they're all going to work."

I nodded toward the sleepy bevy of middle-aged men as they converged upon the boat in business suits and brash neck ties, the young women dressed as their doubles in androgynous navy-blue double-knits, with Nikes slipped over their nylons.

"You know damn well what I mean." Dad halted for a moment at the hatch to steal a scanning glance of the wharf. "Jack London worked right here, you realize."

"Sure, Dad."

"He was a sailor and an oyster pirate," rhapsodized my father, "and then he started arresting his oyster pirate pals when that turned out to be a better job."

"You've told me, Dad."

"He didn't take the day off whenever he felt like it."

The ferry rocked hard, broke from its moorings, and glided into the channel. It took about fifteen minutes to run the full distance through Oakland's harbor to the mouth of the bay, including one stop in Alameda. The thick and bilgy water looked like a reservoir of green ink.

"Didn't you ever take a day off?"

"Labor Day and Christmas."

We passed through a forest of masts, the harbor's small stand of yachts docked alongside the plasterboard abutment of restaurants, bars, and motels bearing Jack London's name; past the warehouse district where railroad tracks inscribed into the hot-tar streets vanished behind the port walls; alongside the navy barges and liver-green Quonset huts settled across from the shoreline's huge mechanical cranes, six-story hoists that looked like faceless white workhorses loading cargo containers aboard immense freighters bearing the names of dead presidents.

On the bow of the second deck, Dad and I lapped up the salt spray like contented spaniels nipping at the wind. The Bay Bridge slashed across the skyline, serving up San Francisco's high-rise spires upon the platter of its fourth and fifth spans. The remainder of the city was wrapped in fog.

"This is where Jack London really started out," said Dad.

"I know."

Facing the open bay, about two hundred yards from the nub of the wharf, the boat jostled atop the waves and the wind slapped our faces with calloused hands. The bay was a wild place, a tempest. Between Oakland and San Francisco, the ferry surged toward the tug of the Golden Gate, skating off toward the crazy ocean that could lead any-where.

My father and I had been talking about Jack London for years. Oak-land's most famous writer was one of our perennial subjects, and our enthusiasm had everything to do with that great American unmention-able—class.

Over time, one way or another, class showed up like a famished uncle at every family argument. It was class that Dad and I both invoked to bind us together, if only by a spider's strand, even while we used it to straight-arm each other into separate corners. As far back as I can remember, it was class that lit the fuse to our competition.

I first heard the word when my fifth-grade teacher unwisely pro-claimed that America was a classless society. It was a silly, popular notion back in the early 1960s, though as school children we were then too young to trace its strands of pretzel logic. Given the ancient sorrows of class-conscious Europe—most of us were scarcely one generation away from immigrant grandparents—it must have seemed like brassy romance and patriotism to brag to a room full of ten year olds that our own young Republic breached no official division of wealth and status. In America, asserted our teacher, we were all middle class.

But when I passed this good news along to my parents over the evening's dinner of hot dogs, canned peas, and mashed potatoes, my father thrust his elbows upon the green Formica kitchen tabletop, squared his head into his outstretched palms, and growled lowly to himself. He still wore the day's working clothes—his coffee-colored Ben Davis trousers, a bleached-bright baby-blue denim shirt rolled up to the throbbing biceps, ankle-high, steel-tipped boots.

"You don't know what you're talking about," my father informed me, scooping mounds of canned peas and mashed potatoes into his hungry mouth.

"But Teacher said."

"Teacher hasn't worked a lick in her life, and don't know what she's talking about either."

On the subject of education, my father would always be seriously divided. He was a high school graduate—but from there on, largely self-educated. He had mastered some practical science and mechanics, and he knew U.S. history very well, familiar with everything that had transpired during his lifetime. Dad was blessed with a rat-trap memory that secured squirming morsels of Kipling, Longfellow, and Shakespeare, which he had recited decades earlier at the head of his one-room country school in Oregon; but formal learning, at every level, aroused his suspicion. When it came time for me to think about college, he was full of impossible advice: *You're a fool,* he tortuously explained, *if you don't get an education so that you can live off the sweat and blood of the people who do the real work in this country!*

Books, however, were a different story.

Shortly after my fifth-grade teacher had theoretically dismantled America's class structure, I recall one Saturday morning when Dad escorted me to the public library and filled my arms with volumes of Jack London, which were, in a sense, my patrimony.

They were all the books Dad had read as a kid. *Before Adam, The Cruise of the Dazzler, Tales of the Fish Patrol.* I pored over them as I would a child's atlas of the world and then plundered the Klondike stories—"To Build A Fire," "An Odyssey of the North," and *Call of the Wild*; and then on to the sailor sagas, starting with *South Sea Tales.* *The Sea-Wolf* was rougher going. Captain Wolf Larsen's own shipboard bookcase was stocked with unfamiliar names and titles: Tennyson, DeQuincey, Bulfinch's *Mythology*, and *The Origin of Species.* But I plodded on, disregarding what I could not comprehend, all for the glimpse contained within those pages of boyish adventure.

What delighted me most, however, was the life behind the stories. I asked my father about Jack London, and he knew everything. London had grown up in Oakland. His mother had been a spiritualist, his father, John Chaney, who never acknowledged him, an itinerant astrologer. As a teenager, he quit school, went to sea, hit the road to join Coxey's army of the unemployed who were marching to Washington to demand jobs, landed in jail in Buffalo, and then lit out for the Yukon gold rush of 1897, only to return one year later from his Klondike stake with $4.50 worth of gold dust in his pockets. But London had also packed back to Oakland a rich trove of frontier lore, and it quickly made him one of the country's most popular and prolific writers.

Jack London wrote fifty books—Dad read them all—and shouldered assignments as a newspaper correspondent covering the Boer War in

South Africa, the Russo-Japanese War, and the Mexican Revolution. He married twice, fathered two daughters, sailed the South Seas on his own yacht, and died at forty. He was the most famous American writer of his time, his own life story wrapped in a flag of self-promoting legends equaled only in our day by the Hemingway myth. To think of him now, as many people do, as the overgrown, scrappy boy of gregarious naivete who wrote some good dog stories and then drank himself to death, is to flit over the impact he had on millions of people, and particularly the country's bright and curious workingmen, who weren't ordinarily engaged with "literature."

Jack London was their spokesman, the first great American myth-maker to insist that the hard grind of a workingman's life might contain lessons for others; that when the workingman's best instincts collided with society's boundaries, the impact could spin him off toward heroic pursuits—that *all* of history's legendary heroes, from Odysseus the sailor to Paul Bunyan the lumberjack, had been tough, thinking, workingmen. London was the model of strong hands and rough wits.

~~~~~~

"Do you remember how you used to lie to me when I was a boy?" I asked my father, as we bobbed upon the San Francisco Bay on the commuter ferry.

Gulls had collected around the stern, fluttering like kites upon the tail breeze. We were gliding toward an unfettered view of the Golden Gate as the suspension beams of the Bay Bridge shivered five hundred feet above us.

"What are you talking about?"

"You told me that Treasure Island was inhabited by pirates."

Treasure Island was the U.S. naval base at the midpoint of the bridge. The island itself was manufactured from twenty million cubic yards of bay silt and landfill piled high for the 1939 San Francisco Golden Gate International Exhibition.

"You claimed," I reminded him, "that every man on Treasure Island wore a patch over his right eye and kept a parrot on his shoulder. You said that if some stranger accidently drove onto the island, the pirates would grab him, saw off his leg, and replace it with a peg."

"I bet that made you think twice about running away from home to join the navy, didn't it?"

"I suppose it did."

"Well, then good. 'A man who calls a spade a spade should be compelled to use one.' I guess I don't have to tell you, that's Oscar Wilde."

We watched the bay waters ruffle and cream up against the ferry's hull until San Francisco was extruded from the mist. A foghorn blasted two times in the distance, and the port veered into view. The hum of the city smothered the sound of the waves splashing against our boat, and I felt sad to be so close to land.

My father and I were spending the entire day together, an event unimaginable in the past. Once, years before, when I asked Dad how he got along with his own father, he swallowed his answer hard and raised his fists to guard his face, pivoting half-circles in a boxer's defensive stance. Between us, too, it was often like that, though without blows. If we were both these days more tolerant of one another, the change was probably due to some inevitability of family geometry that neither of us had the insight or perspective to fully grasp. Fathers and sons never conform into a single shape; rather, they seem drawn from their first meeting as separate lines whose faulty parallelism is revealed only over the years as they exhibit an infinitesimal quiver toward each other arching across the page—and at some point, these two lines may intersect. Perhaps we were now at that point.

I knew that our intimacy had been rekindled by reading the right book at the right time. In this case, the book was *Martin Eden*, Jack

London's autobiographical novel tracing the immense hard work of a young sailor who educates himself to become a writer.

Martin Eden is not one of the books my father pressed upon me as a kid. And it's far from London's best. But reading it for the first time this year I felt connected to all the romance and tragedy that lies at the heart of any early struggle for learning. Unlike Dad's favorite London novel—*The Star Rover*, which portrays the unshackling of a convict's imagination from Folsom solitary through some quirky means of astral projection, the dreamer loosened from his limits to experience an eternity of reincarnated adventures—*Martin Eden* doesn't promise freedom for the workingman. In the end, its disillusioned hero drowns himself.

And still, Martin Eden *is* Jack London—a more romantic version, surely, swollen through poetic exaggeration, though recognizable yet as a "work beast, shot through with stray flashes of divinity," the partisan of "stokeholes and forecastles, camps and beaches, jails and boozing-kens, fever-hospitals and slum streets." When Martin Eden meets the comely sister of a better educated and far daintier young man whom Eden rescues from a street-brawling bully, he is entranced instantly by the young girl's mannered beauty *and* her volume of Swinburne on the drawing room table. It's one of literature's most unlikely seductions: the first stanzas of the decadent English poet, read aloud by the privileged young girl, ignite within Martin Eden a commitment to let learning transform him. "He had caught a glimpse," explains the author, "of the apparently illimitable vistas of knowledge."

Like Martin Eden—like my father—Jack London bore upon his back the full load of contradictory attitudes about learning and labor.

"*All my days I have worked hard with my body,*" London explained in a 1903 essay entitled "How I Became a Socialist" (which aimed to clarify why he began much of his voluminous correspondence with the salutation, "Dear Comrade," and concluded, "Yours for the Revolution"), "*and according to the number of days I have worked, by just that much am I nearer the bottom of the Pit. I shall climb out of the Pit, but not by the muscles of my body shall I climb out. I shall do no more hard work, and may God strike me dead if I do another day's hard work with my body more than I absolutely have to do.* And I have been busy ever since running away from hard work."

As a young man, London ran straight to the Oakland Public Library. There he investigated William Morris, Marx, Mill, Ricardo, Adam Smith, Proudhon, Saint-Simon, Fourier—and with the inevitable crankiness of the autodidact, Madame Blavatsky and Herbert Spencer. London pored over the dictionary, adding twenty words each day to his vocabulary. Like Caliban, he had purloined the rulers' books, leafing madly through their pages for the secrets that enslaved him. Ricocheting with giddy energy between visions of class solidarity and the bombastic pride of the self-proclaimed workingman's aristocrat—a kind of Horatio Alger Jacobin—London stood upon his soapbox in the triangular park banking Oakland's old city hall and preached revolutionary aims until he was arrested. He ran three times for mayor of Oakland under the Socialist banner—earning 245 votes in 1901; losing the election to a wealthy populist, who had once hired his stepfather, John London, as a strikebreaker.

What lay behind this drive for reconstructing his life? Not the will to power, not the winning of the girl; it was the man's ocean of curiosity. Jack London—like my father, like Martin Eden—had, in the words of his biographer Andrew Sinclair, "the vaunting ambition of the self-taught; he was always the poor boy in the public library who determines to read every book on every shelf in order to add up the whole sum of human knowledge. It was a noble and futile aspiration, and a tragic one." Tragic because it led to "an infinite dissatisfaction," the envy that knotted up Caliban's entrails—a risk borne by every young working person who dares to dip into borrowed books.

When I think of my father and *his* books, I sense curiosity's same treacherous appeal. In our family, curiosity stirred up weird and stubborn argument. When my mother's sisters would visit from the East Coast, Dad urged that their immigrant Italian family must have once marched with Garibaldi's red legions against the Pope in Rome. (Nobody seemed to get it. Was their sister's husband joking, was he nuts? Who was Garibaldi?) Dad buzzed off to the living room bookshelf to select Volume G of *The World Book Encyclopedia*. Then he leafed merrily through its pages until he located Garibaldi's wizened portrait. Evidence. The world was full of histories and plots whose surface we can barely skim. Of course, while Garibaldi marched, my mother's ancestors were all fishing quietly off the coast of Calabria. But the sheer proximity of encyclopedic knowledge stirred my father; reference books containing the near-sum of human endeavor *were sitting in his living room*!

My father didn't start reading until he fell off his bicycle at the age of fourteen and broke his leg in two places below the knee. Since Dad couldn't move his leg all summer to work or play, he retreated into books. For the first time, he read Zane Grey, J. W. Schultz's Indian stories, most of Edgar Rice Burroughs, James Olivier Curwood's *Nomads of the North*, and Jack London. By the time his leg had healed, there was no place that he couldn't travel, if he could only locate the right book. Fifteen years later, Dad contracted tuberculosis and sat out World War II. He was expected to die, but stubbornly pulled through. Part of the cure was the hospital library, his one ticket beyond the terminal ward. During those three years in the TB sanatorium, my father pored over the day's newspapers and scoured the popular magazines and pulps—*Life*, *Collier's*, *Black Mask* (the last then filled with the fledgling stories of Chandler and Hammett); he read all of Upton Sinclair and Sinclair Lewis and whatever Zane Grey, Edgar Rice Burroughs, or Jack London he hadn't yet mastered—and finally, those volumes of history, social theory, and mythology crammed into Wolf Larsen's shipboard bookshelf. Like the star-roving convict of his favorite London fantasy, my father saw once again that there was a world swung open to him like a castle gate that he might enter whenever the demands of his working life temporarily receded.

But while experience showed him that reading was good for a workingman, he still had to wonder what purpose it served?

Books were finally the province of people who didn't have to work for a living, an unthinkable circumstance for him. By "work," I mean— and he meant—work hard, until you *sweat*. My father had justified his entire life through labor, working with his hands. I remember as a child touching his hands—that fleshy, familiar pair of weathered work gloves. I ran my small fingers along their cracked-dry rivulets, drawing circles around the calloused peaks. Lizard skin. Leather. Hands may not record the full measure of a life, but they contain crucial data on how each day is consumed. Hands marking time like toppled tree trunks, ring after ring. One way or another, all the men in my family earned a living with their hands.

Until I came along.

~~~~~~

From the San Francisco side of the bay, Oakland is barely visible, a grey miniature settled upon the flat water. San Francisco has always played Emerald City to Oakland's Kansas, with the Bay Bridge spanning the distinction. But for people far from either place, the winning city is not always obvious.

A few years ago, my friend Mitchell met some young Russians in Vienna who were fanning out through Europe at the first break of perestroika. When the Russians quizzed my friend about his home in America, Mitchell explained that he hailed from the nation's most beautiful city—San Francisco.

"San Francisco," pondered one Russian. "Is that anywhere near Oakland?"

"Well, yes," answered Mitchell, "it's right across the bay. But most people usually think that San Francisco is really—"

"*Oakland!*" the Russian exclaimed rapturously, "I have heard about it all my life. I would love to see Oakland some day before I die. Please," he whispered into Mitchell's ear with a hush of wonderous expectation, "*tell me all about Oakland!*"

For decades, Jack London was the most widely read American author in the Soviet Union. (Will this still be true as the cult of the worker dissolves into the vagaries of the marketplace?) Trotsky proclaimed London a prophet superior to Rosa Luxemburg. As Lenin was dying, his wife, Krupskaya, read aloud Jack London's short story "Love of Life," the terrifying tale of a lost and starving prospector who drags himself across the Arctic tundra, wrestles to the death a lone sick wolf and finally, somehow, survives.

Though often sentimental in the brooding Russian fashion, London is still the spokesman for the quintessential American port town—tough, prevailing, desperate enough to assume the risks of the indifferent ocean.

"Oakland is the best city," I proclaimed to my father, as our ferry approached San Francisco. The salt air was rank and cold, the sky rolled down like a grey curtain.

"I can't see why you even live there," said Dad, now the complete suburbanite. He had never romanticized city life, and now he read newspaper accounts daily of Oakland's crime and decay—so why try to fool him?

"Home of the Hell's Angels," I insisted, "birthplace of the Black Panthers. We've got a pretty good baseball team, too. Oakland is better than San Francisco because San Francisco is much too exceptional." It was the usual second-city argument, erected upon a bedrock of sophistry. But even as I uttered these words—Oakland as paradise, rather than as eyesore—they sounded ridiculous. It was childish comfort that I drew by arguing that I fit better than my father in Jack London's city.

"Personally," insisted Dad, a master of contrariness, "I wouldn't mind seeing the whole place burn down. Probably will."

When I was in my early twenties, I argued with similar contrariness that I should be counted as one of my family's workingmen. I was finishing college, and, between dropping in and dropping out, I took the usual laboring jobs then available to skill-less young men, imagining that some brief tenure inside a factory or warehouse would entitle me to retain the language of my family. At Christmas we'd all gather around the dinner table, carve the turkey, drink the good bourbon, and chat up the classic working-class family concerns. There would be talk of overtime and RIFs, mandatory graveyard and swingshift, bonuses and layoffs—and then, as the best bourbon welled up and overflowed into early evening resentment, somebody would defiantly assert that the country would never be fit until working people trimmed the excesses of the rich, even if it meant plucking the rich out of their homes in the hills by the sharp creases of their starched collars. It always boiled down to what you could accomplish with your own hands.

But I didn't work with my hands. Or at least, I wouldn't be working with my hands forever, which everybody at the table except me understood.

My own home was becoming exotic. I wasn't working class. I'd only grown up there.

And although my father and I might read the same books, finding some momentary agreement in the real and imagined adventures of other men, we could never read these books in precisely the same way. This is one of the fundamental sorrows of fathers and sons whose lives must diverge once they continue past the point of intersection.

Yet how I longed to belong there, amid the comfort of hard work and bitterness—and how much more desperately I wanted to escape.

During these years—my mid-twenties, Dad's early sixties—it seemed the only books that my father and I could honestly share were the torn and grease-spattered repair manuals that governed our wheezing old automobiles. How many hours did we spend together fixing the family cars—two hundred, five hundred, one thousand? One of us would buy another clunker, and then we'd struggle to repair it in Dad's garage over the noise of sputtering engines and our own breathy curses.

"What do you think?" I'd ask my father, after pulling my old wreck of an ancient Dodge station wagon into his driveway for the ritual tune-up.

"Well, I can say this. It's a heap."

"Four wheels," I argued. "Good spare in the trunk. So far, she starts right up on a cold morning."

"Well," said Dad, "we'll see."

I would pop the hood, and he'd sink his scarred hands into the heart of the machine, twisting, tightening, demanding a small tool whose name I could never remember, and with one arm jutting out from underneath the engine, he would fiddle with all of the car's hidden imperfections. When he finished, he'd glide over to the wash basin, cleaning himself by rote with a tub of lanolin soap, hand over hand over hand.

"I forget," I asked, eager to prolong the encounter. "How do you set the timing exact if the crankshaft pulley isn't marked?"

Grease and suds of creamy lanolin ran down my father's overalls and splashed across the concrete floor.

"There's always going to be some kind of mark on the crankshaft pulley," he instructed. "A notch, a light groove, something. Right?"

"Right."

"So what you do is take a tape and measure your pulley's diameter, then multiply that by the number of degrees advance setting that your service manual recommends. Does that make sense to you?"

I nodded.

"You got to know that. If you're really interested in getting it exact, you got to have some basic information. And you can't be lazy about looking it up," he insisted. "If you got the book, you got to look it up."

"And so that gives you the number of inches that you turn the crank-shaft from Top Dead Center."

"Correct."

There is really very little that needs to be said about the malfunctioning and repair of automobiles, yet throughout these years we seemed to say it all—shoptalk being the only talk.

And then, quite suddenly, I found that my car had lost much of its usefulness—at least, I couldn't use it to get myself out of Oakland. It wasn't that the car no longer worked; we kept it running just fine. Rather, one day in my mid-twenties I simply woke up stone-terrified to drive my old clunker, or anybody's car, over bridges. A great unreasonable fear, a phobia. In particular, when I crossed the Bay Bridge to San Francisco, my hands froze around the steering wheel, I flushed with cold sweat and my heart pounded like two fists beating against the inside of my chest trying to get out. It was silly, humiliating, inexplicable.

But the symbolism couldn't have been more obvious. In the San Francisco Bay Area—Oakland especially—if you don't cross bridges, there isn't any place to go. I was stuck one place, unable to cross over. It's not that I needed to give up Oakland for San Francisco (I really preferred the East Bay, I did!), but I required mobility. I was yearning for the larger world beyond my family—and yet languishing for want of the simple courage to navigate over bridges that were less concrete and iron than incomplete aspirations and misfired starts.

As a boy, Jack London found the route to his new life on the ocean. He sailed off from Oakland with the oyster pirates, through the Golden Gate as a ship's mate, prospector, and adventurer; and he returned home sufficiently swept away from his roots to remake himself into a writer. Upon the bow of his own ship—as a boy, his cherished *Dazzler;* as the wealthy author, the illustrious and doomed *Snark*—he faced the mouth of the Pacific, invigorated by its wind-snap cold and inscrutable opportunities. The Golden Gate could lead anywhere; there was no swifter, stronger, more perilous current any place between the West Coast and Japan. Like every young romantic, Jack London understood in his blood that the ocean could destroy him or fashion him into something entirely unexpected—and it did both. London was drawn to oblivion. He wanted to erase his life, wash away the past. And yet that was an impossible task. He would always cling to what he had been.

"While I cultivate new classes," London once told a friend, "I hate to be out of grip with the old."

As the ferry hitched up to the dock, Dad and I watched the passengers bumble down the gangplank, draining the boat like an empty wine bottle. Everybody was scurrying off to work, except us. Dad didn't want to get off.

"Why should we?" he demanded. "We don't have to go anywhere. We can just pay our way and go back."

"You mean you want to turn around and go home?"

"Well, we came for the ocean, didn't we? I want to see more of it."

We stood at the bow, silently inspecting the rest of the bay. To the west, Alcatraz and Angel Island were merely peaks in the fog. The ferry's engine started up again for the return trip, and Dad pointed out to me that Marin had vanished entirely.

We passed under the Bay Bridge like a dream.

It took me several years to drive fearlessly over bridges, though even now I'll occasionally feel the electric twinge of recollected anxiety as my car rolls toward the crest of the Bay Bridge's cantilever, and the magnificent prospect of San Francisco breaks into view like an ivory wave. It simply took time. By the end of my twenties, I had fallen in love and made new friends, but most of all I'd embarked upon life as an adult by working each day in ways that nobody could mistake for my father's workingman's life, ways that even—do I dare say this?—*aspired* to be middle class.

It would be attractive to say that my own working life is now at bottom no different, certainly, no better, than my father's work history, but I know otherwise. The freedom of one generation is purchased by another's labor, and it would be a sin to disregard any improvements, and therefore, the sacrifice. My father's life and mine are not interchangeable, and I'll always mourn the distance between them. But in truth, I can now only imagine the distance.

As we rode the ferry back to Oakland, lurching into a tail wind and sailing straight into a perfect day, I felt once again the exhilaration of crossing the bay, and I was thankful for this watery connective tissue that would always bind together our worlds. In the distance, Oakland's downtown offices shone dully, like blocks of chalk, and the wind roared us back home.

"Do you feel like you've seen enough of the world," I asked my father upon the windy bow of the ferry. Oakland's skies were sheer blue, rippling with the rainbow effluence of its industrial breeze.

"Of course not," he said. "I hardly got started."

"Then where would you still like to go? You can go anywhere from here," I reminded him.

"No place," he said. "You go."

San Francisco blew at our backs—and the working people of the East Bay that Jack London had known, and my father had labored among, and I had left, slowly drew into view. They bustled together, swirling into the city's marvelous hodge-podge, living the adventures that somebody else was now preparing to tell.